ROBERT D. MURPHY

A REGISTER OF HIS PAPERS

IN THE HOOVER INSTITUTION ARCHIVES

COMPILED BY

GRACE M. HAWES

HOOVER INSTITUTION

STANFORD UNIVERSITY

1989

This work was made possible through a gift from the Corning Glass Works Foundation, Corning, New York.

The Hoover Institution on War, Revolution and Peace, founded at Stanford University in 1919 by the late President Herbert Hoover, is an interdisciplinary research center for advanced study on domestic and international affairs in the twentieth century. The views expressed in its publications are entirely those of the authors and do not necessarily reflect the views of the staff, officers, or Board of Overseers of the Hoover Institution.

Hoover Press Bibliography 73

Copyright 1989 by the Board of Trustees of the Leland Stanford Junior University

All rights reserved. No part of this publication may be reproduced, stored in a retrieval system, or transmitted in any form or by any means, electronic, mechanical, photocopying, recording, or otherwise, without written permission of the publisher.

First printing, 1989.

Manufactured in the United States of America.

Library of Congress Cataloging-in-Publication Data

Hoover Institution on War, Revolution, and Peace.
   Robert D. Murphy : a register of his papers in the Hoover Institution archives.

   (Hoover Press bibliography ; 73)
   Includes index.
   1. Murphy, Robert D. (Robert Daniel), 1894- --Archives--Catalogs. 2. Hoover Institution on War, Revolution, and Peace--Archives--Catalogs. 3. United States--Foreign relations--20th century--Sources--Bibliography--Catalogs. I. Hawes, Grace M. II. Title. III. Series.
Z6616.M945H66 1989 [E748.M875]   016.32773 89-15410
ISBN 0-8179-2732-8

CONTENTS

Foreword..i

Biographical note.......................................iv

Series description......................................vi

Container list

    Biographical File....................................1

    Speeches and Writings File...........................3

    Early Career File...................................21

    Envoy to North Africa File..........................22

    Political Adviser File..............................26

    Ambassadorships, Department of State File...........33

    Later Years File....................................38

    Oversize File.......................................58

    Phonotapes..59

    Photographs...59

Index...60

Robert D. Murphy as Deputy Under Secretary of State, ca. 1956

FOREWORD

From humble beginnings, Robert D. Murphy became one of America's leading diplomats and statesmen. In a distinguished public service career that lasted almost sixty years, Ambassador Murphy had the good fortune to serve in interesting places at interesting times. He also had the good judgment to preserve the records of his extraordinary experiences, records that now constitute the Robert D. Murphy Collection at the Hoover Institution Archives.

One of Murphy's first diplomatic posts, in the early 1920s, was Vice Consul in Munich, where he reported to Washington on the rise of national socialism and where he lived across the street from the Nazi leader, Adolf Hitler. Throughout the 1930s, he served as Consul in Paris. When German troops entered the city in June 1940, Murphy met with the German commanding general in order to safeguard American and French interests. Later that year, he was appointed Charge d'Affaires at Vichy.

Shortly thereafter, President Franklin Roosevelt chose Murphy to be his special envoy to French North Africa. Roosevelt, realizing the vital role that French North Africa could play in the war, wanted a trusted personal representative to investigate conditions and report back directly to him. Robert Murphy proved the wisdom of Roosevelt's choice when his careful negotiations laid the groundwork for the successful Allied invasion of North Africa in 1942. The Murphy Papers for this period include communications with President Roosevelt and other wartime leaders, memoranda from American Ambassador to Vichy William Leahy, military and secret service (Office of Strategic Services) reports of Allied operations, as well as the diplomatic records of the wartime conferences of Allied leaders at Casablanca and Cairo.

Murphy continued his service in Africa as political adviser under General Dwight D. Eisenhower until 1944, when he was sent to Italy as American Ambassador on the Advisory Council to the Allied Control Commission. In his new post, he participated in the signing of the Italian armistice. Murphy's intimate involvement with the Allied high command laid the basis for his subsequent memoirs, <u>Diplomat Among Warriors</u> (1964).

His next assignment took him to Germany as a member of the Office of Military Government, which was set up to administer postwar reconstruction. During these years, he also served on American delegations to the Councils of Foreign Ministers in

Moscow, London, and Paris, and to the Tri-Partite Talks. The records of these conferences, including the most secret negotiations, reports, memoranda and correspondence are part of the Murphy Papers. There are as well rare captured German documents, including transcripts of wartime conferences of Hitler with his top military commanders.

In 1949, Robert Murphy was appointed United States Ambassador to Belgium and, in 1952, the first American postwar Ambassador to Japan. During his tenure in Tokyo, he also acted as Political Adviser to the United Nations Command in connection with the negotiations on the Korean War armistice. From 1953 to 1959, his assignment to the Department of State involved him in negotiations with leaders in many parts of the world: Tito in Yugoslavia, Saeb Salam in Lebanon, Bourguiba in Tunisia and King Hussein in Jordan. Shortly before he retired from government service in 1959, he served as Under Secretary of State. Records of Murphy's many important assignments during these years appear in his papers.

After his retirement, Murphy began a new career as an executive with Corning Glass International where he successfully combined his new duties with his role as elder statesman. He served on the Foreign Intelligence Advisory Board during the Kennedy, Johnson and Nixon administrations, as well as on the Intelligence Oversight Board and the Commission on the Organization of the Government for the Conduct of Foreign Policy. Memoranda, reports and internal communications from these many significant assignments appear in the Murphy papers.

The vast correspondence Murphy carried on throughout his life is of equal importance to historians. There are letters to and from a wide assortment of important people: world leaders Andrei Vyshinsky, Harold Macmillan and Konrad Adenauer; Presidents Franklin Roosevelt, Harry Truman and Dwight Eisenhower; Secretaries of State James Byrnes, Cordell Hull, Dean Acheson and John Foster Dulles; French military leaders Charles de Gaulle, Maxime Weygand, Henri Giraud and Jean Darlan; movie actors Douglas Fairbanks and Adolphe Menjou, and violinist Yehudi Menuhin.

The register to the Robert D. Murphy Collection is composed of four parts. A Biographical Note (p. iv) indicates important dates in the course of Murphy's career. The overall structure of the collection is outlined in the Series Description (p. vi), which explains its major divisions. The Container List (beginning on p. 1) describes in detail the materials within each series. An Index (beginning on p. 60) provides a single alphabetical listing of all access points in the register with page references.

A few items in the papers retain national security classifications. Until such time as they can be declassified, they have been withdrawn from the collection and their withdrawal is so noted in the register.

The Robert D. Murphy Papers, a gift to the Hoover Institution Archives by his daughters, Rosemary Murphy and Mildred Pond, in 1978, are open to the public without charge. The Archives Reading Room is open on weekdays from 8:15 a.m. to 4:45 p.m. For further information, please contact Hoover Institution Archives, Stanford University, Stanford, California, 94305.

I am especially pleased to acknowledge the generous financial support of the Corning Glass Works Foundation, Corning, New York, without which the preparation and publication of this guide would not have been possible.

                Charles G. Palm
                Associate Director, Hoover Institution

ROBERT D. MURPHY

BIOGRAPHICAL NOTE

1894, October 28	Born, Milwaukee, Wisconsin
1917-1919	Clerk, American Legation, Bern, Switzerland
1920	LL.B., George Washington University
1921	Married, Mildred Taylor Vice Consul, Zurich, Switzerland
1921-1925	Vice Consul, Munich, Germany
1925	Consul, Seville, Spain
1928	LL.M., George Washington University
1926-1930	Department of State, Washington, D.C.
1930-1940	Consul, Paris, France
1940	Charge d'affaires, Vichy, France
1940-1942	Presidential envoy to French North Africa
1941	Concluded economic accord with General Maxime Weygand
1942	Effected preparations for Allied landings in North Africa
1942-1944	Chief Civil Affairs Officer and Political Adviser on Staff of Supreme Commander Co-chairman, North African Economic Board
1942-1943	Member, Advisory Council, Allied Control Commission for Italy
1944-1949	U.S. Political Adviser, Germany
1949	Director, Office for Germany and Austria, Department of State
1949-1952	Ambassador to Belgium

1952-1953	Ambassador to Japan
1953	Assistant Secretary of State for United Nations Affairs
1953-1959	Deputy Under Secretary of State
1959	Under Secretary of State for Political Affairs Retirement from government service
1960-1978	Successively President, Chairman of the Board, and Honorary Chairman of the Board, Corning Glass Works, Corning Glass International
1964	Author, <u>Diplomat Among Warriors</u>
1968-1969	Member, Presidential Transition Committee
1973-1975	Member, Commission on the Organization of the Government for the Conduct of Foreign Policy
1969-1976	Member (Chairman, 1976), Intelligence Oversight Board Member, President's Foreign Intelligence Advisory Board
1978, January 9	Died, Washington, D.C.

ROBERT D. MURPHY PAPERS

Box Nos.	Series Description
1-18.	BIOGRAPHICAL FILE, 1913-1971. This file contains personal materials, including awards, citations, appointment books, clippings, honorary degrees and souvenirs; arranged by physical form.
18-42.	SPEECHES AND WRITINGS, 1937-1977. Handwritten, typewritten, and printed copies of speeches and writings by Robert Murphy with related notes and research materials; arranged chronologically.
43.	EARLY CAREER, 1922-1940. Memoranda, correspondence, subject files from Robert Murphy's career as a foreign service officer in various posts; arranged chronologically.
44-52.	PRESIDENTIAL ENVOY TO FRENCH NORTH AFRICA AND POLITICAL ADVISER (overlapping assignments), 1940-1944. Correspondence, reports, memoranda, and office files from Robert Murphy's years as President Franklin D. Roosevelt's special envoy to French North Africa and political adviser to General Dwight D. Eisenhower in the Allied Force Headquarters, Algiers and Caserta; arranged by form or function. This series also contains files from Murphy's appointment with the Allied mission with General P.A. Mason Macfarlane and as a member of the American delegation to the Malta Conference, the Casablanca Conference, the Cairo Conference and the Teheran Conference. In 1943, Murphy was also appointed to serve on the Allied Advisory Council for Italian and Balkan Affairs.
53-77.	POLITICAL ADVISER, 1944-1949. Memoranda, correspondence, reports, office files, and printed material from Robert Murphy's service as political adviser, Office of Military Government, United States (OMGUS); arranged by form or function.
78-92.	AMBASSADORSHIPS, DEPARTMENT OF STATE, 1949-1959. Correspondence, memoranda, reports, and subject files collected by Robert Murphy during his tenure as Director, Office for Germany and Austria, Department of State; Ambassador to Belgium; Ambassador to Japan; Assistant Secretary of State for United Nations Affairs; Deputy Secretary of State; and Under Secretary of State for Political Affairs; arranged by form.

93-143.	LATER YEARS, 1959-1978. Correspondence, memoranda, reports, and office files from Robert Murphy's career as a business executive. Correspondence related to his appointment to the Presidential Transition Committee, 1968-1969, and office files from the Commission on the Organization of the Government for the Conduct of Foreign Policy, 1973-1974, are also included in this series; arranged by form or function.
144-146.	OVERSIZE FILE. Albums of clippings about Robert Murphy, 1949-1951; photo album; memorabilia, and various oversized materials.
Tape Cabinet	PHONOTAPES. 5 reels.
	PHOTOGRAPHS (1,298 prints), 1920-1975.

```
CONTAINER LIST:
Box    Folder
No.    No.
-----------------------------------------------------------------------
1.             BIOGRAPHICAL FILE, 1913-1971
                    Appointment books, schedules
       1-8                1946-1953

2.     1-5                1953-1954

3.     1-7                1955-1956, September

4.     1-7                1956, October - 1958, July

5.     1-7                1958, August - 1959

6.     1-2                1968-1969
       3-4          Awards
       5            Biographical data
                    Career records.  Assignment records, promotion notices,
                         travel orders, organization charts, and
                         correspondence related to the career of Robert Murphy
       6                  1913-1919
       7                  1920
       8                  1921
       9                  1922
       10                 1923
       11                 1924

7.     1-2                1925
       3                  1926
       4                  1927
       5                  1928
       6                  1929
       7                  1930
       8                  1931
       9                  1932
       10                 1933
       11                 1934
       12                 1935
       13                 1936
       14                 1937
       15                 1938

8.     1                  1939
       2                  1940
       3                  1941
       4                  1942
```

8 (Contd.)		BIOGRAPHICAL FILE (Contd.)
		Career records (Contd.)
	5	1943
	6	1944
	7	1945
	8	1946
	9	1947
	10	1948
9.	1-2	1949
	3	1950
	4-5	1951
	6-8	1952
	9	1953
	10	1954
	11	1960
	12	1961-1967
10.		Clippings about Robert D. Murphy
	1	1920
	2	1925
	3	1926
	4	1930-1931
	5	1939
	6	1941
	7	1942
	8	1943
	9	1944
	10	1945
	11	1946
	12	1948
	13-17	1949
11.	1	1950
	2	1952
	3	1954
	4	1956
	5	1957
	6-11	1958
12.	1-3	1958
	4	1959
	5	1960
	6	1961
	7-8	1962
	9	1963
	10	1964
	11	1965
	12	1966
	13	1967
	14	1968
	15	1970
	16	1971

13.　　　　　　　　BIOGRAPHICAL FILE (Contd.)
　　1-2　　　　　　Education. Papers related to Robert Murphy's candidacy
　　　　　　　　　　　for a Master of Laws Degree from George Washington
　　　　　　　　　　　University, 1927-1928
　　3　　　　　　　Family clippings
　　4　　　　　　　Coat of arms
　　5　　　　　　　Family memorabilia
　　6-7　　　　　　Guest lists
　　8　　　　　　　Health. Physical examination records
　　9-10　　　　　Honorary degrees
　　11-12　　　　　Household expenses, personal effects, employees

14. 1-10　　　　　Household expenses, etc.

15. 1-9　　　　　　Household expenses, etc.

16. 1-2　　　　　　Household expenses, etc.
　　3　　　　　　　Identity cards
　　4　　　　　　　Interview. List of questions for Robert Murphy from
　　　　　　　　　　　Grand Hebdomadaire Illustre, July, 1943
　　5　　　　　　　Invitations, calling cards, laissez passers
　　6-9　　　　　　Miscellany

17. 1　　　　　　　Miscellany
　　2-8　　　　　　Souvenirs. Programs, brochures, guest lists

18. 1-2　　　　　　Telephone directories
　　3-5　　　　　　Travel orders
　　6　　　　　　　Trip notes, February, 1941
　　　　　　　　　SPEECHES AND WRITINGS, 1937-1977
　　7　　　　　　　Notes, n.d.
　　8　　　　　　　"The Utility of a Permanent and Trained Foreign
　　　　　　　　　　　Service", n.d. Handwritten draft
　　9　　　　　　　"Income Tax Returns", The American Foreign Service
　　　　　　　　　　　Journal, September, 1937. 1 printed copy
　　10　　　　　　　Remarks at the University Club of Paris, May 2, 1939.
　　　　　　　　　　　Correspondence, 3 carbon copies
　　11　　　　　　　Remarks at the American Club of Paris, July 20, 1939. 3
　　　　　　　　　　　carbon copies

19. 1　　　　　　　Research materials, 1941
　　2-3　　　　　　Research materials, 1944-1945
　　4　　　　　　　Notes for public remarks, ca. 1944
　　5　　　　　　　Remarks on the Mediterranean Theater, Council of Foreign
　　　　　　　　　　　Relations, New York, January 27, 1944. Typescript
　　　　　　　　　　　copy
　　6　　　　　　　Notes on remarks made to French Military Government
　　　　　　　　　　　students, Paris, December 15, 1944. Typescript copy
　　　　　　　　　　　in French
　　7　　　　　　　"The American Military Policy Towards Germany", December
　　　　　　　　　　　16, 1944. Correspondence, typescript, carbon copies,
　　　　　　　　　　　draft

19 (Contd.)		SPEECHES AND WRITINGS (Contd.)
	8	Remarks to French Military Government officers, Paris, February 7, 1945. Typescript copy in French
	9	Remarks on Political Affairs, Paris, February 14, 1945. Outline, typescript copy
	10	"Germany and Democracy", Military Government Conference, Frankfurt, August 17, 1945. Program, typescript copy
	11	Remarks to American correspondents, December 11, 1945. Typescript copy
	12-15	Research materials, 1946
20.	1	"Foreign Policy", written for <u>Berlin Post,</u> February 4, 1946. Correspondence, carbon copy
	2	Remarks, Bremerhaven, May 11, 1946. Carbon copy
	3	Remarks on the German Occupation, August 21, 1946. Typescript copy
	4	Remarks on U.S. Policy, October 24, 1946. Carbon copy
	5	Research materials, 1947
	6	Remarks at dedication of synagogue, Munich, May 20, 1947. Draft
	7	Notes for Berlin seminar, May 28, 1947. 2 carbon copies
	8	Commencement address, Roberts High School, Berlin, July 11, 1947. Notes, typescript and carbon copies
	9	Remarks to Syracuse University alumni, Berlin, August 17, 1947. Outline
	10	"Murphy Stresses Importance of Spiritual Values in Reconstruction of Germany", interview, December 15, 1947. Printed copy
	11-12	Research materials, 1948
	13	"Foreign Policy", ca. 1948. Notes, outline
	14	Remarks on Germany, ca. 1948. Typescript copy
	15	Remarks on postwar Germany, ca. 1948. Typescript copy
	16	Remarks at commencement, institution unknown, ca. 1948. Handwritten copy
	17	"The United States Views Germany's Democratization", ca. 1948. Carbon copy
	18	Remarks to American Women's Club, Berlin, January 6, 1948. Typescript copy
	19	Remarks on Germany, Louisville, Kentucky, February 10, 1948. Typescript copy
	20	"The Ruhr and Security", May 20, 1948. Carbon copy
	21	Commencement address, Roberts High School, Berlin, June 15, 1948. Carbon copy
	22	Notes, drafts, 1949
	23	Research materials, 1949
	24	Remarks on the German problem, National Advertising Council, Washington, D.C., February 9, 1949. 4 carbon copies
	25	Remarks on Germany delivered by Robert Murphy on behalf of the Secretary of State, Washington, D.C., March 30, 1949. Typescript copy
	26	"The Role of the Political Adviser to the Military Governor", National War College, Washington, D.C., October 17, 1949. Printed copy, carbon copy

21.		SPEECHES AND WRITINGS (Contd.)
	1-2	Research materials, 1950
	3	Remarks, January 13, 1950. Carbon copy
	4	Remarks at the Belgian-American Association luncheon, Brussels, January 25, 1950. 4 typescript copies (2 in English, 2 in French)
	5	Remarks at a reception for the mayor and aldermen, Antwerp, January 27, 1950. 2 typescript copies (1 in French, 1 in English)
	6	Remarks at the Cercle Industrielle et Commerciale, February 9, 1950. Typescript
	7	Remarks, Military Order of Foreign Wars, February 14, 1950. 2 carbon copies
	8	Remarks, Brussels Chamber of Commerce, February 20, 1950. 4 typescript copies (2 in English, 2 in French)
	9	Remarks, George Washington's Birthday dinner, February 25, 1950. Typescript, carbon copy
	10	Remarks, Cercle Gaulois, Brussels, March 15, 1950. 2 typescript copies (1 in French, 1 in English), memorandum
	11	Remarks, American-Belgian Association, March 24, 1950. 2 typescript copies (1 in English, 1 in French)
	12	Remarks, American Club of Paris, March 30, 1950. 2 typescript copies
	13	Remarks at Zeebrugge, May 12, 1950. 2 typescript copies (1 in English, 1 in French)
	14	Remarks, May 23, 1950. Carbon copy
	15	Remarks, Memorial Day, May 30, 1950. 3 typescript copies (2 in English, 1 in French)
	16	Remarks, Jesus College, Oxford, July 2, 1950. 2 typescript copies
	17	Remarks, Bastogne Memorial, July 16, 1950. 4 typescript copies (2 in French, 2 in English)
	18	Remarks, Foire de Gand (Ghent Fair), September 18, 1950. 2 drafts, 5 typescript copies (2 in English, 2 in French, 1 in Dutch)
	19	Remarks, Polytechnic Institute, Mons, and the Belgian-American Association, November 28, 1950. 4 typescripts (2 in French, 2 in English)
	20	Remarks, Cercle Mars et Mercure, December 7, 1950. 3 typescript copies (2 in French, 1 in English), carbon copy
22.	1	Notes, drafts, 1951
	2-4	Research materials, 1951
	5	Remarks, American Chamber of Commerce, January 16, 1951. Typescript, carbon copy
	6	Remarks, American Club luncheon. 2 typescript copies, 2 press releases
	7	Remarks, Royal Automobile Club, February 12, 1951. 2 typescript copies (1 in English, 1 in French)
	8	Remarks, University of Louvain, February 13, 1951. 2 typescript copies (1 in English, 1 in French)

22 (Contd.)		SPEECHES AND WRITINGS (Contd.)
	9	Remarks, George Washington's Birthday Dinner, February 23, 1951. 2 typescript copies (1 in French, 1 in English)
	10	Remarks, Flemish Economic Association, April 16, 1951. 3 typescript copies (1 in English, 1 in French, 1 in Flemish)
	11	Remarks, Third Liege International Fair, April 23, 1951. 2 typescript copies (1 in English, 1 in French)
	12	Remarks, Brussels Fair, April 27, 1951. 2 typescript copies (1 in French, 1 in English)
	13	Remarks, Belgian-American Association, May 28, 1951. 2 typescript copies (1 in French, 1 in English)
	14	Remarks, Waereghem, June 3, 1951. 2 typescript copies (1 in English, 1 in French)
	15	Remarks, Ghent Fair, September 18, 1951. 3 typescript copies (1 in English, 1 in French, 1 in Flemish)
	16	Remarks, American Club of Brussels, September 20, 1951. 3 typescript copies (1 in English, 1 in French, 1 in Flemish)
	17	Remarks, Virginia Women's Forum, Richmond, Virginia, November 8, 1951. 4 typescript copies (2 in French, 2 in English)
	18	"The United States and West European Unity", National Foreign Trade Council, New York, December 7, 1951. Typescript, draft
23.	1	Research materials, 1952
	2	"Political Factors in War", National War College, Washington, D.C., January 7, 1952. Typescript
	3	Remarks, American Club, Belgium, January 24, 1952. Typescript, press release
	4	Remarks, Grandes Conferences Catholique, Charleroi, January 25, 1952. 2 typescript copies (1 in English, 1 in French)
	5	Remarks, Societe d'Economie Politique, Fondation Universitaire, Brussels, January 29, 1952. 2 typescript copies (1 in English, 1 in French), press release
	6	Remarks, American Chamber of Commerce, February 5, 1952. Typescript, draft
	7	Remarks, American Club of Antwerp, February 22, 1952. Typescript
	8	Remarks, University of Liege, March 4, 1952. 2 typescript copies (1 in French, 1 in English)
	9	Transcript of telecast on Belgium, April 6, 1952. Carbon copy
	10	Remarks on arrival in Japan, April 21, 1952. Carbon copy
	11	"The Soldier and the Diplomat", Foreign Service Journal, May 1952. Printed copy
	12	Remarks at the signing of the Tripartite Fisheries Convention, May 9, 1952. Printed copy

23 (Contd.)   SPEECHES AND WRITINGS (Contd.)
   13   Remarks, American-Japan Society, May 29, 1952. Carbon copy
   14   Remarks, Seiwa Kai Society of Tokyo, June 10, 1952. Typescript
   15   Remarks, Tokyo Chamber of Commerce and Industry, June 16, 1952. Typescript, carbon copy, memorandum, press release
   16   Remarks, American Chamber of Commerce, Tokyo, June 24, 1952. Typescript, press release
   17   Remarks, Haneda, July 1, 1952. Typescript, carbon copy
   18   Remarks, Ochanomizu University, Tokyo, July 11, 1952. Typescript, press release
   19   Remarks, Black Ships Festival, July 15, 1952. Typescript, press release
   20   Remarks, American-Japan Society of Kobe, July 16, 1952. Carbon copy
   21   Remarks, Osaka, July 17, 1952. Press release
   22   "Japan and Free Asia", American Japan Society, September 1952. Carbon copy
   23   Remarks at the presentation of American law books to the Supreme Court of Japan, September 2, 1952. Press release
   24   Remarks, United Nations Association of Japan, September 24, 1952. Typescript, press release
   25   Remarks, Second World Conference of Buddhists, Tokyo, September 25, 1952. Press release
   26   Remarks, Rotary Club of Tokyo, October 22, 1952. Press release
   27   Research materials, 1953
   28   Remarks on presentation of quota visa, January 21, 1953. Typescript
   29   Remarks, American Club, Tokyo, January 20, 1953. Typescript
   30   Remarks, National 4-H Club Congress, Tokyo, March 18, 1953. Press release
   31   Remarks on presentation of Encyclopedia Americana to International Christian University, April 17, 1953. Press release
   32   Remarks, American-Japan Society, Tokyo, April 24, 1953. Printed copy
   33   Remarks, Chronoscope Program, August 21, 1953. Typescript, carbon copy, correspondence
   34   Remarks, American Association for the United Nations, September 13, 1953. Draft, notes
   35   Remarks, St. Matthew's Church, October 11, 1953. Typescript, memorandum
   36   Remarks, John Carroll Society, October 11, 1953. Printed copy, correspondence
   37   Remarks, <u>New York Herald Tribune</u> Forum, October 18, 1953. Printed copy
   38   Remarks, Mayor's reception, Philadelphia, October 23, 1953. Carbon copy

23 (Contd.)   SPEECHES AND WRITINGS (Contd.)
  39   "The Role of the United States", speech, World Affairs Council, Philadelphia, October 23, 1953. Printed copy, typescript, press release
  40   Remarks, Navy League of the United States, October 26, 1953. Carbon copy, draft, correspondence
  41   "The United States Looks at the United Nations", speech, Convention of the Texas Congress of Parents and Teachers, San Antonio, November 19, 1953. Press release, correspondence
  42   Remarks, Oklahoma City Chamber of Commerce, November 20, 1953. Outline, correspondence
  43   Remarks, Notre Dame New York President's Committee, December 9, 1953. 2 carbon copies, correspondence

24. 1   Notes, 1954
  2-3   Research materials, 1954
  4   Remarks, American Foreign Service Association, January 1954. 2 printed copies in <u>Foreign Service Journal</u>
  5   WITHDRAWN. SECURITY CLASSIFIED MATERIAL
  6   Remarks, American Foreign Service luncheon, National Press Club, January 18, 1954. Typescript, carbon copy, news clipping
  7   Remarks, Harvard Law School Association, January 20, 1954. Draft, correspondence
  8   Remarks, Cardoza Foundation, Philadelphia, January 26, 1954. Typescript, carbon copy, draft, correspondence
  9   Remarks, University Club of New York, January 30, 1954. 2 carbon copies, correspondence
  10   "Brotherhood in the World of Today", speech, National Conference of Christians and Jews, New York, February 4, 1954. Carbon copy, press release, correspondence
  11   Remarks, Marquette Alumni Reception, National Press Club, Washington, D.C., February 24, 1954. Typescript, carbon copy
  12   Remarks, National Education Association, March 7, 1954. Notes, correspondence
  13   "America, Japan and the Future of the Pacific", speech, World Affairs Council of Northern California and the American Legion, March 8, 1954. Typescript, carbon copies, press release
  14   "Europe Is Important", speech, Town Hall Businessmen's Luncheon, Los Angeles, March 9, 1954. Typescript, carbon copy, press release, correspondence
  15   "Some Problems of American World Relations", speech, World Affairs Council of Los Angeles, March 9, 1954. Typescript, carbon copy, correspondence, program
  16   Remarks, Japan Society Dinner, New York, March 18, 1954. Typescript, carbon copy, press release, correspondence
  17   Remarks, West Point Founder's Day dinner, New York, March 20, 1954. Carbon copy, memoranda

24 (Contd.)   SPEECHES AND WRITINGS (Contd.)
- 18   Remarks, American Society of Newspaper Editors, Washington, D.C., April 17, 1954. Typescript, carbon copy, correspondence
- 19   Remarks, Knights of Columbus Pan American Dinner, Washington, D.C., April 29, 1954. Typescript
- 20   Remarks, United Defense Fund, April 29, 1954. Typescript, correspondence
- 21   Remarks, Massachusetts Committee, Catholics, Protestants and Jews, Boston, May 6, 1954. Typescript, correspondence, memorandum
- 22   Remarks, Inter-American Bar Association of the Bar Association of the District of Columbia, May 18, 1954. 2 carbon copies, correspondence

25. 1   WITHDRAWN. SECURITY CLASSIFIED MATERIAL
- 2   Commencement address, Fordham University, New York, June 9, 1954. Correspondence, press release, program
- 3   "The United States and the Uncommitted World", speech, Zionist Organization of America, New York, June 24, 1954. 3 carbon copies, press release, correspondence
- 4   Remarks, annual convention of Air Force Association, August 20, 1954. Typescript, press release, correspondence. Typescript of remarks on accepting Association Medal for Secretary of State John Foster Dulles
- 5   WITHDRAWN. SECURITY CLASSIFIED MATERIAL
- 6   Remarks, President's Committee on Employment of the Physically Handicapped, August 26, 1954. Typescript, 2 partial carbon copies, correspondence
- 7   Remarks, American Association for the United Nations, September 13, 1954. Press release
- 8   Remarks, United States Naval Academy, Annapolis, Maryland, October 7, 1954. Typescript, carbon copy
- 9   Remarks at the rededication of the Foreign Service Memorial Plaque, October 11, 1954. 2 carbon copies, correspondence
- 10   Remarks, Business Advisory Council, Hot Springs, Virginia, October 23, 1954. Typescript, carbon copy, correspondence
- 11   "The Defense of Asia", speech, National Foreign Trade Convention, November 16, 1954. Typescript, press relase, correspondence
- 12   Remarks, Armed Forces Staff College, December 9, 1954. Typescript, 2 carbon copies, correspondence

26. 1   Notes, 1955
- 2   Research materials, 1955
- 3   Remarks, testimonial luncheon for Matthew Woll, January 8, 1955. Typescript, carbon copy, memoranda, press release, correspondence
- 4   Remarks, Australian-American Society dinner in honor of Prime Minister Menzies, March 7, 1955. Typescript, carbon copy, memorandum, correspondence

26 (Contd.)   SPEECHES AND WRITINGS (Contd.)

    5   Remarks, fourth International Trade Fair, Seattle, Washington, March 11, 1955. Typescript, press release, memorandum, correspondence

    6   Remarks, Oak Ridge Institute of Nuclear Studies, Oak Ridge, Tennessee, April 10, 1955. Typescript, memorandum, correspondence

    7   Remarks, "On Wisconsin" Award, Department of State Auditorium, Washington, D.C., April 15, 1955. Press release, correspondence

    8   Remarks, International Chamber of Commerce, Washington, D.C., April 20, 1955. Typescript, carbon copy, memorandum

    9   "Collective Security in the Air Age", *Annals of The American Academy of Political and Social Science,* May 1955. Printed copy

    10   Remarks, Chamber of Commerce of the United States, Washington, D.C., May 2, 1955. Typescript, press release, clipping

    11   Remarks, Foreign Service Institute, May 2, 1955. Memorandum

    12   "Our Policies in Asia", speech, Foreign Policy Association, Pittsburgh, May 5, 1955. Typescript, press release, memorandum, correspondence, clipping

    13   Remarks, Rockford Chamber of Commerce, Rockford, Illinois, May 24, 1955. Typescript, carbon copy, memorandum, correspondence

    14   Testimony before the Senate Foreign Relations Committee on the Geneva Conventions for the Protection of War Victims, June 3, 1955. Carbon copy, draft

    15   Remarks at the presentation of the Laetare Medal to Ambassador Jefferson Caffrey, Notre Dame University, June 5, 1955. Typescript, message from Secretary of State John Foster Dulles, memorandum, draft

    16   Commencement address, Georgetown University, June 6, 1955. Typescript, printed copy, correspondence, carbon copy

    17   "United States Diplomacy", commencement address, Marquette University, Milwaukee, Wisconsin, June 8, 1955. 2 typescript copies, printed copy, 2 carbon copies, memorandum, correspondence

    18   Remarks on television program, "Youth Wants to Know" with Konrad Adenauer, June 14, 1955. Carbon copy

    19   Remarks, Indiana University Conference on Problems of American Foreign Policy, Bloomington, June 25, 1955. Typescript, carbon copy, press release, memoranda

27. 1   Remarks, Washington-Rochambeau Celebration, Newport, Rhode Island, July 9, 1955. Typescript, carbon copy, printed copy, correspondence, memorandum

    2   Statement before the House Foreign Affairs Committee on NATO Status of Forces Treaty, July 19, 1955. Press release, memorandum

27 (Contd.) SPEECHES AND WRITINGS (Contd.)
- 3   Statements for Voice of America. Pakistan International Industries Fair, September 2, 1955. Typescript. Salonika, Greece International Trade Fair, September 4, 1955. Typescript
- 4   Remarks, Canada-United States Conference, University of Rochester, Rochester, New York, September 1, 1955. Two carbon copies, press release, memorandum, program, correspondence
- 5   Remarks, National Sales Executives, Washington, D.C., September 8, 1955. Carbon copy, correspondence
- 6   Remarks, International College of Surgeons, Philadelphia, September 15, 1955. Typescript, press release, agenda, correspondence
- 7   Remarks, European-American Discussion Group, Garmisch, Germany, September 23, 1955. Memoranda, correspondence
- 8   Remarks, Chamber of Commerce, Danville, Illinois, November 2, 1955. 2 carbon copies, memorandum, correspondence
- 9   Remarks, Committee on Foreign Affairs, Cleveland, Ohio, November 3, 1955. Partial typescript, carbon copy, correspondence, memorandum
- 10   Remarks, Supreme Lodge of B'nai B'rith, Washington, D.C., November 7, 1955. Typescript, press release, memoranda, correspondence
- 11   "Africa and Asia in the World Community", speech, Catholic Association for International Peace, Washington, D.C., November 12, 1955. Typescript, press release, memorandum, correspondence
- 12   "The Principle of Self-Determination in International Relations", Department of State Bulletin, November 28, 1955. Printed copy
- 13   Testimony before the Senate Judiciary Committee Hearings on Trading with the Enemy, November 29, 1955. Press release
- 14   Remarks, Seton Hall University, South Orange, New Jersey, December 8, 1955. Carbon copy, press release, memorandum
- 15   Research materials, 1956
- 16   Remarks, Pennsylvania Bar Association, Harrisburg, Pennsylvania, January 20, 1956. Typescript, press release, memorandum, correspondence
- 17   Remarks, Dartmouth Club of Washington, February 7, 1956. Typescript, carbon copy, correspondence
- 18   Remarks, Newman Club Convention, New York, February 12, 1955. 2 carbon copies, memorandum, correspondence
- 19   Remarks, Washington Conference of Mayors, February 16, 1956. Printed copy, notes, correspondence
- 20   "For a Better World", Department of State Bulletin, March 5, 1956. 2 printed copies

28.   SPEECHES AND WRITINGS (Contd.)
  1. Remarks, George Washington Alumni Luncheon, March 24, 1956. Typescript, press release, correspondence
  2. Remarks, The Christophers, March 27, 1956. Correspondence
  3. Remarks, Symposium on NATO, College of William and Mary and the Norfolk, Virginia Chamber of Commerce, April 2, 1956. Press release, memorandum, correspondence
  4. Remarks, American Society of Newspaper Editors, April 19, 1956. Press release
  5. Remarks, Manhattanville College, May 1, 1956. Typescript
  6. Remarks, sixth annual World Affairs Forum, Foreign Policy Association of Pittsburgh, May 2, 1956. Typescript, press release, correspondence, clippings
  7. Remarks, citizenship ceremonies, May 8, 1956. 2 carbon copies, correspondence
  8. Remarks, Father's Club of the College of New Rochelle, New York, May 13, 1956. Carbon copy, memorandum, correspondence
  9. Remarks, Maxwell Air Force Base, Alabama, May 14, 1956. Typescript, correspondence
  10. Remarks, United States Committee for the United Nations, May 15, 1956. Typescript, carbon copy
  11. Remarks, University of Chicago Club, Washington, D.C., May 23, 1956. Carbon copy, correspondence
  12. Statement before House Subcommittee on Government Operations, May 31, 1956. Press release
  13. Remarks, Army War College, Carlisle Barracks, Pennsylvania, June 6, 1956. Typescript, memorandum, correspondence
  14. Statement on the President's Special International Program, June 14, 1956. Mimeograph copy
  15. WITHDRAWN. SECURITY CLASSIFIED MATERIAL
  16. "Soviet Developments and Their Meaning for U.S. Foreign Policy", statement before the House Foreign Affairs Committee, October 11, 1956. Typescript, carbon copy
  17. Remarks, Institute of International Affairs, University of Washington, October 24, 1956. Typescript, press release, memoranda, correspondence, 2 carbon copies
  18. "Berlin, Symbol of Free-World Determination", Department of State Bulletin, October 29, 1956. Printed copy, 2 carbon copies, clipping, correspondence
  19. Remarks, United States Delegation to the 11th United Nations General Assembly, November 9, 1956. Typescript
  20. Remarks, American-Jewish Joint Distribution Committee, New York, November 29, 1956. Typescript, carbon copy, printed copy, memorandum, correspondence

29.
  1. Notes, 1957
  2. Research materials, 1957
  3. Remarks, America-Italy Society dinner, January 15, 1957. Typescript, carbon copy, memoranda, correspondence

29 (Contd.)   SPEECHES AND WRITINGS (Contd.)
   4   Remarks, Brussels Fair luncheon, January 24, 1957. Outline, correspondence
   5   Remarks as participant, Bilderberg Group Conference, February 15-17, 1957. Memoranda, correspondence, program, background information
   6   Remarks, presentation of film Weltschmerz, February 20, 1957. Typescript
   7   Remarks, Diplomatic and Consular Officers, Retired (DACOR), February 21, 1957. Typescript, correspondence
   8   Statement to the House Foreign Affairs Subcommittee on Europe, March 6, 1957. Typescript, carbon copy, memorandum
   9   Remarks, The Citadel, March 8-9, 1957. Typescript, memorandum, correspondence
  10   Statement on the President's Special International Program, House Appropriations Committee, March 13, 1957. Typescript
  11   "The United States Looks at the Middle East", speech, Georgetown University, March 14, 1957. Typescript, press release, correspondence
  12   Statement before the Subcommittee on the Armed Services, Senate Foreign Relations Committee, March 18, 1957. Typescript, carbon copy, draft
  13   Statement on passport policy, Senate Foreign Relations Committee, April 2, 1957. Press release, correspondence
  14   "Building for Peace", speech, tenth annual Conference on World Affairs, University of Colorado, April 4, 1957. Typescript, memorandum, correspondence, program
  15   Remarks, Foreign Relations Commission of the American Legion, April 25, 1957. Typescript, carbon copy
  16   Remarks, Catholic Women's Club, New Rochelle, New York, April 28, 1957. 2 carbon copies, memorandum, correspondence
  17   Remarks, National Council of Catholic Men, Cincinnati, Ohio, May 11, 1957. Typescript, press release, program, background information, memorandum, correspondence
  18   Commencement address, Catholic University of America, Washington, D.C., June 9, 1957. Typescript, press release, correspondence
  19   Commencement address, University of Pittsburgh, June 12, 1957. Typescript, carbon copy, draft, correspondence, memoranda, clipping

30. 1   Statement, House Armed Services Committee on H.R. 8704 (Exercise of Foreign Criminal Jurisdiction over Members of the Armed Forces Serving Overseas), July 26, 1957. 2 carbon copies
   2   WITHDRAWN. SECURITY CLASSIFIED MATERIAL

30 (Contd.)		SPEECHES AND WRITINGS (Contd.)
	3	Remarks, annual Conference of U. S. Mayors, September 9, 1957. Typescript, press release, memorandum, correspondence
	4	Remarks to the United States Delegation to the 12th United Nations General Assembly, September 13, 1957. Outline
	5	Remarks, 175th anniversary of the Great Seal, September 16, 1957. Typescript
	6	Remarks, United Givers Fund Appeal, September 23, 1957. Typescript
	7	Remarks, American representatives of the World Veterans Federation, October 4, 1957. Outline
	8	Remarks, Mid-Career Class, Foreign Service Institute, October 4, 1957. Outline
	9	Remarks, Business Advisory Council, October 25-26, 1957. Notes, outline, correspondence, memoranda
	10	WITHDRAWN. SECURITY CLASSIFIED MATERIAL
	11	"Some Major Aspects of Current Foreign Policy", speech, Non-Governmental Organizations Conference on Foreign Policy, December 9, 1957. Typescript, carbon copy
	12	Notes, 1958
	13	Research materials, 1958
	14	"Diplomats and Soldiers", <u>Federalist,</u> Fall, 1958. 2 printed copies, correspondence, draft, press release
	15	Remarks, Veterans of Foreign Wars, February 3, 1958. Draft
	16	Remarks, Council on Foreign Relations, Chicago, February 21, 1958. Memoranda, correspondence
	17	Statement, Senate Committee on Foreign Relations on recent incidents in South America, Lebanon, and elsewhere, May 19, 1958. 3 typescript copies
	18	Remarks, Department of State Auditorium, May 22, 1958. Typescript
	19	Remarks, Colgate University Foreign Policy Conference, July 1, 1958. Typescript, press release, correspondence, memorandum
	20	Remarks, St. Stanislaus Retreat League, Cleveland, September 28, 1958. Carbon copy, correspondence, memorandum, clipping, program
31.	1	Remarks, Catholic Lawyers Guild, October 1, 1958. Press release, correspondence, clipping
	2	"Academic Training and Career Diplomacy", speech at the dedication of the Edmund A. Walsh Memorial Building, Symposium on Foreign Service, Georgetown University, Washington, D.C., October 13, 1958. Typescript, carbon, press release, correspondence
	3	Remarks, Business Advisory Council, Hot Springs, Virginia, October 18, 1958. 2 carbon copies, correspondence, memoranda
	4	Remarks, Senior Foreign Service Officers Course, Foreign Service Institute, October 21, 1958. Outline, correspondence

31 (Contd.)   SPEECHES AND WRITINGS (Contd.)
   5   Remarks, Chicago Advertising Council, October 23, 1958. 2 typescripts, 2 carbon copies, correspondence, memoranda
   6   Remarks, Catholic Association for International Peace, Washington, D.C., October 25, 1958. Typescript, press release, correspondence
   7   Remarks, Milwaukee County war memorial, November 11, 1958. Typescript, press release, correspondence, memoranda
   8   Remarks, 45th National Foreign Trade Convention, New York, November 17, 1958. Typescript, carbon copy, press release, memoranda, correspondence
   9   Remarks, A. and H. Kroeger Dinner Forum, New York, December 2, 1958. Typescript, 2 carbon copies, correspondence, memoranda
  10   "The Strategy of Communist Advance", speech, Commonwealth Club, San Francisco, December 12, 1958. Typescript, 2 carbon copies, memoranda, correspondence, press release
  11   Remarks, American Committee on Italian Immigration, December 20, 1958. Typescript, carbon copy, memoranda, correspondence

32. 1   Remarks, World Affairs Council, Philadelphia, January 23, 1959. Press release, correspondence, memoranda
   2   "American Foreign Policy Is Your Business", speech, Economic Club of Detroit, January 26, 1959. Typescript, press release, correspondence, clippings, memoranda, carbon copy, program
   3   Remarks, Worcester Economic Club, Worcester, Massachusetts, February 10, 1959. 2 carbon copies, press release, memoranda, correspondence
   4   Remarks, National Industrial Conference Board, February 19, 1959. Carbon copy, outline, correspondence, prospectus, memoranda
   5   Remarks, Treasury Department Conference, February 25, 1959. Carbon copy, correspondence, memoranda
   6   "The World Political Situation", speech, National War College, Washington, D.C., March 18, 1959. Typescript, correspondence
   7   Remarks, Japan-America Society, March 25, 1959. Carbon copy, press release, correspondence
   8   Remarks, Religion in American Life, Inc., April 13, 1959. Press release, memoranda, correspondence
   9   Remarks, Notre Dame Club of Chicago, April 13, 1959. Press release, correspondence, memoranda
  10   Remarks, Bellarmine College, Louisville, Kentucky, May 13, 1959. Carbon copy, press release, memoranda, correspondence, program
  11   Remarks, World Refugee Year, May 22, 1959. Memoranda
  12   "International Political Situation", Secretaries Conference, June 26, 1959. Typescript, photocopy, correspondence

32 (Contd.)		SPEECHES AND WRITINGS (Contd.)
	13	Remarks, Boys Nation, July 21, 1959. Draft
	14	Remarks, World Confederation of Organizations of Teachers, Washington, D.C., August 6, 1959. Carbon copy, press release, correspondence
	15	Remarks, Military Assistance Institute, Washington, D.C., August 7, 1959. Correspondence
	16	Remarks, Passport Legislation Hearing, August 11, 1959. Typescript
	17	Remarks, School of Banking, University of Wisconsin, August 27, 1959. Correspondence, background information
	18	Television interview, September 11, 1959. Typescript
	19	Remarks, Foreign Service Association, September 25, 1959. 2 carbon copies
	20	Remarks, Ernst Reuter stamp ceremony, Post Office Department, September 29, 1959. Carbon copy
33.	1	Remarks, Conference on Business Outlook in the Middle East, Johns Hopkins School of Advanced International Studies, October 6, 1959. 2 carbon copies
	2	Remarks, International Labor Organization Dinner, October 9, 1959. 3 carbon copies
	3	"The Shape of American Policy", speech, Institute of World Affairs, October 20, 1959. Press release, memorandum
	4	"United States Foreign Policy in Europe", speech, The National Women's Republican Club, New York, October 22, 1959. Press release, memoranda
	5	Remarks, Conference of National Organizations, November 5, 1959. Typescript, 2 carbon copies, correspondence
	6	"Cultural Values in a World of Change", speech, dedication of the Pius XIII Memorial Library, St. Louis University, November 23, 1959. Carbon copy, correspondence
	7	"What Is Past Is Prologue", speech, National Press Club, Washington, D.C., December 1, 1959
	8	"State's Good and Faithful Servant," Washington Post, May 29, 1960. Review of Katherine Crane, Mr. Carr of State. Printed copy
	9	Statement as personal representative of the President of the United States and chief of the American delegation to the independence ceremonies of the Congo on his arrival in Leopoldville, June 29, 1960. 2 typescript copies, 1 in English, 1 in French
	10	Review of Roscoe Drummond and Gaston Coblentz, Duel at the Brink, July, 1960. Typescript
	11	Notes for remarks at Japan Society dinner for Prince Akihito and Princess Michiko, September 30, 1960. Typescript and holograph
	12	Remarks at the Morgan Guaranty Trust Company dinner, October 3, 1960. Typescript

33 (Contd.)   SPEECHES AND WRITINGS (Contd.)
   13   "Public Understanding: Foundation for Defense," General Electric Defense Quarterly, October-December, 1960. Printed copy
   14   Address at Commencement, Boston College, June 12, 1961. 2 typescripts, 3 programs, 1 printed copy, 1 printed copy from the Congressional Record
   15   Remarks at American Research Hospital in Poland dinner, 1962. Typescript
   16   "Story of How Berlin Became the World's No. 1 Danger Spot", U.S. News and World Report, April 9, 1962. Printed copy
   17   Remarks at National Conference of Christians and Jews dinner honoring General Lucius D. Clay, June 18, 1962. Typescript, guest list
   18   Address. October 2, 1962. Typescript
   19   Remarks at Japan American Society, October 4, 1962. Typescript
   20   Remarks at the Commercial Club of Boston, March 20, 1963. Typescript
   21   Remarks at the Corning Seminar on Glass Ceramics, June 6, 1963. Typescript
   22   Address on United Nations Day, Martinsburg, West Virginia, October 24, 1963. Typescript
   23   Notes for remarks at National Conference of Christians and Jews dinner, November 19, 1963. Typescript, program

34.   Diplomat Among Warriors, Garden City, New York: Doubleday and Company, Inc., 1964.
   1   Correspondence, 1965-1969
   2-6   Research materials, notes
   7-8   Draft

35. 1-9   Drafts, Chapters 10-30

36. 1-10   Drafts, Chapters 14-22

37. 1-6   Drafts, Chapters 23-26

38. 1-8   Drafts, Chapters 27-29

39. 1   Remarks at Marquette University dinner, March 5, 1964. Typescript
   2   Miscellaneous notes, April 9, 1963
   3   Remarks at Cincinnati Chapter of the National Conference of Christians and Jews, May 18, 1964. Typescript
   4   Review of John Paton Davies, Foreign and Other Affairs, June, 1964. Typescript, correspondence
   5   Remarks on Burke Wilkinson, Night of the Short Knives, July 14, 1964. Typescript, correspondence

39 (Contd.)   SPEECHES AND WRITINGS (Contd.)
   6   "Some Aspects of American Foreign Policy", speech, Graduate School of Banking, University of Wisconsin, Madison, Wisconsin, August 18, 1964. 2 printed copies, typescript
   7   Remarks about Ambassador Amory Houghton, Corning Glass Works Service Dinner, September 12, 1964. Typescript
   8   Review of Dean Acheson, Morning and Noon, Chicago Tribune, October 8, 1964. Typescript
   9   "Some Aspects of American Foreign Policy", speech, Los Angeles, California, November 8, 1964. Typescript
   10   "American European Cooperation", This Europe, February, 1965. Printed copy, correspondence
   11   Review of Milton Viorst, Hostile Allies: FDR and de Gaulle, New York Times Book Review, February 21, 1965. Printed copy, correspondence
   12   Address to the 13th annual citation dinner, National Conference of Christians and Jews, May 6, 1965. Typescript
   13   Interview on John Foster Dulles, Oral History Project, Princeton University, May 19 and June 8, 1965. Typescript, correspondence
   14   Remarks at the Toledo Council on World Affairs, September 22, 1965. Typescript
   15   "Reminiscences of a Diplomat", 19th annual Conference of Bank Correspondents, November 22, 1965. Typescript
   16   Remarks at the National Industrial Conference Board, December 16, 1965. Typescript
   17   Foreword to Mose L. Harvey, East West Trade and United States Policy, 1966. Photocopy
   18   Remarks on the Merv Griffin Show, March 16, 1966. Typescript, correspondence, contracts
   19   Statement to the Committee on Foreign Affairs, House of Representatives, May 25, 1966. 2 typescripts, printed copy, correspondence
   20   "Reflections on Our World Position", speech, Rockhurst College commencement, Kansas City, Missouri, May 29, 1966. Printed copy, 2 typescripts, correspondence, clippings, program
   21   Review of William Withers, Freedom Through Power, Chicago Tribune, June 12, 1966. Printed copy, typescript, correspondence

40. 1   Remarks, National Security Agency Week, September 23, 1966. 3 typescripts, correspondence, clipping
   2   "Some Thoughts on Our International Position", speech, World Affairs Council, April 17, 1967. 2 typescripts, correspondence, notes
   3   "Thoughts on Our International Position", speech, Harvard Club of Washington, D.C., April 27, 1967. 3 typescripts, correspondence, printed copy in the Congressional Record
   4   Review of Vladimir Petrov, Money and Conquest, May 16, 1967. 2 typescripts, correspondence

40 (Contd.) SPEECHES AND WRITINGS (Contd.)
- 5   "The Responsibility of the Business Man in the Community", speech, XXI Congress, International Chamber of Commerce, May 17, 1967. Typescript
- 6   Remarks at luncheon honoring Rabbi Philip S. Bernstein, June 5, 1967. Typescript, correspondence
- 7   Remarks at the Church of the Epiphany, New York, October 8, 1967. Typescript, correspondence
- 8   Remarks at dinner honoring The Prime Minister and Mrs. Eisaku Sato, November 16, 1967. Typescript, correspondence
- 9   Review of Smith Simpson, Anatomy of the State Department, Annals of the American Academy of Political and Social Science, February, 1968. Typescript, correspondence
- 10   Remarks at the Milwaukee County Historical Society, April 18, 1968. Typescript, correspondence, clippings, program
- 11   Remarks at the National Conference of Christians and Jews, May 8, 1968. 3 typescript copies
- 12   "A View of Our World Position", speech, Marquette University commencement, June 2, 1968. 3 typescript copies, correspondence
- 13   Remarks at the Japan International Christian University Foundation, June 17, 1968. 5 typescript copies, correspondence
- 14   Remarks to the National Association of Manufacturers, September 10, 1968. 2 typescript copies, correspondence, printed material
- 15   Statement endorsing Richard M. Nixon for President, October 21, 1968. Typescript, correspondence, clippings
- 16   Remarks at the National Conference of Christians and Jews, November 17, 1968. 2 typescripts, correspondence, program
- 17   Remarks at the New York Building Congress, February 25, 1969. 2 printed copies, 6 typescript copies, correspondence
- 18   Review of Alan Lloyd, Franco, July 10, 1969. 2 typescript copies, correspondence
- 19   "Reflections on Viet Nam", speech, Graduate School of Banking, Madison, Wisconsin, August 19, 1969. 2 typescript copies, correspondence
- 20   Foreword to John R. Beal, Marshall in China, October 20, 1969. 2 typescript copies, correspondence

41. 1   "Japanese American Trends", Pacific Community, April 1970. 2 typescript copies, draft, correspondence.
- 2   Remarks at the Corning Production Club, April 28, 1970. Typescript
- 3   Untitled draft on Southeast Asia, July 15, 1970. Handwritten copy

41 (Contd.) SPEECHES AND WRITINGS (Contd.)

4   "Sino-American Crises in the 1950's", Interview with J.H. Kalicki, July 21, 1970. Typescript, draft, correspondence

5   Review of Richard Hanser, <u>Putsch,</u> August 26, 1970. 2 typescript copies, correspondence

6   Remarks at dinner following the dedication of the Cornelia and Edward Thompson Wailes College Center, Sweet Briar College, October 16, 1970. Typescript, correspondence, notes

7   Remarks at the National Conference of Christians and Jews, October 12, 1971. 2 typescript copies

8   Review of Philip Taft, <u>In Defense of Freedom: American Labor and Foreign Affairs,</u> February 25, 1972. Typescript

9   "The Effects of the International Political Scene on the Multinational Corporation", speech, Corning International Company, directors meeting, October 25, 1972. Typescript

10   Remarks on the presentation of the National Conference of Christians and Jews Brotherhood Award, November 16, 1972. Typescript

11   "The Middle East and North Africa", 1973. 2 typescripts

12   Remarks to welcome Helmut Schmidt, Cosmos Club, January 9, 1973. 2 typescript copies

13   Remarks at the National Conference of Christians and Jews, November 18, 1973. 2 typescript copies, correspondence, program

14   Remarks at the France America Society, March 21, 1974. Typescript, printed material

15   Remarks on receipt of the Sylvanus Thayer Award, United States Military Academy, West Point, May 7, 1974. 3 typescript copies, correspondence, including letters of congratulations, clippings, guest list

16   Remarks at memorial service for Chiang Kai-shek, April 16, 1975. Typescript

17   Remarks at World Affairs Council of Philadelphia, September 11, 1975. Typescript, correspondence

18   Remarks at luncheon for Mr. Soichi Yokoyama, September 30, 1975. Typescript

19   "Notes on Congress and Foreign Policy", speech, Brookings Institute Seminar, November 12, 1975. Typescript

20   Remarks at the National Conference of Christians and Jews, November 23, 1975. Typescript, correspondence

21   Remarks at Special Symposium Commemorating the Twentieth Anniversary of the Hungarian Revolution, George Washington University, October, 1976. Typescript, correspondence, program

22   "Foreign and Military Intelligence", speech, World Affairs Council, Grand Rapids, Michigan, October 4, 1976. 3 typescript copies, correspondence, itinerary

41 (Contd.)   SPEECHES AND WRITINGS (Contd.)
   23   Remarks at George Washington Law Association Founders Day Dinner, November 12, 1976. Typescript, correspondence
   24   Eulogy for Robert D. McClintock, December 1, 1976. Typescript
   25   Statement on Far East-America Council, December 15, 1976. Typescript

42. 1-2   Remarks at the Foreign Policy Association Dinner for Henry Kissinger, January 11, 1977. Typescript, program, itinerary, correspondence
   3-5   Remarks on receipt of William J. Donovan Award, May 18, 1977. Typescript, correspondence, clippings, program
   6   Remarks at the Brook Club Dinner, November 1, 1977. Typescript, correspondence

43.   EARLY CAREER, 1922-1940
                Correspondence, 1924-1934
                    General
   1   undated
   2   1926
   3   1934
   4   Carr, Wilbur, 1924-1925
   5   Cherrington, Edwin, 1933
   6   Rhoade, Max, 1931-1934
            Subject file. Correspondence, memoranda, printed material, reports, 1922-1928
   7   Bavaria. Reports on politics and government, 1923-1925
   8   Chinese Immigration Act of 1924. Instruction from Charles E. Hughes to American diplomatic and consular officers, February 25, 1925
   9   Dakar. Bulletin d'Informations des Troupes, "L'Aggression de Dakar", September 20, 1940
   10   Foreign Commerce Service. A bill introduced into the House of Representatives to establish a Foreign Commerce Service of the United States, January 3, 1924
   11   Foreign service. Correspondence, memorandum and printed material on various aspects of the foreign service
   12   George Washington's Birthday Celebration. Proclamations, correspondence, program clipping, 1925, 1928
   13   German-French Armistice Agreement, June 22, 1940
   14   Miscellany
   15   Prohibition
   16   U.S. - Economic relations - Germany. Reports on American shipping, promotion of trade, 1922, 1924

43 (Contd.)   ENVOY TO NORTH AFRICA, 1940-1944
              Correspondence
              General

	17	1940
	18	1941
	19-21	1942
44.	1-2	1943
	3-5	1944
	6	Alverson, Lyle, 1943
	7	Anslinger, H.J., 1944
	8	Baruch, Bernard M., Jr., 1943
	9	Bertrand-Vigne, Georges, 1940
	10	Boisson, Pierre, 1941
	11	Brewster, Ralph O., 1943
	12	Brown, Lestrade, 1943
	13	Bullitt, William C., 1944
	14	Chapin, Mrs. James P., 1944
	15	Clark, Mark W., 1943
	16	Clarke, Brien, 1943-1945
	17	Cole, Felix, 1943
	18	Crowley, Leo, 1944
	19	Culbert, Frederick P., 1943-1944
	20	Culbertson, Paul, 1943
	21	Davis, Monnett B., 1944
	22	Davis, Norman, 1943
	23	Dawson, William, 1942-1943
	24	Donovan, William J., 1943
	25	Dunn, James C., 1943-1944
	26	Eisenhower, Dwight D., 1942-1944
	27	Erhardt, John G., 1944
	28	Farish, Paul, 1943
	29	Forrestal, James, 1944
	30	Fullerton, Hugh S., 1944
45.	1	Giraud, Henri, 1942
	2	Gruenther, Alfred M., 1943
	3	Guichard, Louis, 1941
	4	Hamilton, Maxwell, 1943
	5	Hayes, Carlton J.H., 1944
	6	Henry-Haye, Pierre, 1941
	7	Herbert, Roscoe, 1944
	8	Hibbard, Frederick, 1942
	9	Holmes, Julius C., 1944
	10	Hoover, Herbert C., 1944
	11	Hrones, John G., 1944
	12	Hull, Cordell, 1940-1944
	13	Huston, Cloyce, 1944
	14	Kirk, Alexander, 1944
	15	Lane, Arthur Bliss, 1943
	16	Leahy, William D., 1942-1944
	17	Lemaigre-Dubreuil, Jacques, 1943

45 (Contd.)		ENVOY TO NORTH AFRICA (Contd.)
		Correspondence (Contd.)
	18	MacArthur, Douglas, II, 1942
	19	Macmillan, Harold, 1943-1944
	20	MacVeagh, Lincoln, 1944
	21	Mallory, L.D., 1944
	22	Marshall, George, 1943
	23	Massigli, Rene, 1943
	24	Mast, Charles, 1944
	25	Matthews, H. Freeman, 1941-1944
	26	Mayer, Ernest de W., 1943
	27	McClure, Robert, 1943
	28	Menjou, Adolphe, ca. 1943
	29	Montrichard, de, 1943
	30	Murphy, Wallace, 1941-1943
	31	Norton, Edward J., 1944
	32	O'Brien, William G., 1943
	33	Offie, Carmel, 1941-1944
	34	Pasquier, Pierre du, 1943
	35	Randshuysen, Gerard, 1943
	36	Reber, Samuel, 1941
	37	Russell, H. Earle, 1941
	38	Russell, Richard, 1943
	39	Schott, William W., 1943
	40	Shaw, G. Howland, 1944
	41	Shirer, William, 1943-1944
	42	Smith, W. Bedell, 1943-1944
	43	Solborg, Robert, 1941
	44	Stephens, Dorsey, 1944
	45	Stettinius, Edward, 1943-1944
	46	Tait, George, 1943
	47	Tuck, S. Pinkney, 1944
	48	Van Heck, Paul, 1944
	49	Vyshinsky, Andrei, 1944
	50	Wasson, Thomas, 1940-1941
	51	Watson, H., 1944
	52	Weygand, Maxime, 1940-1942
	53	Winant, John, 1944
46.		Office file, Presidential Envoy and Political Adviser. Memoranda, correspondence, printed material, reports, 1940-1944
	1	Allied operations, December, 1941-July, 1942
	2	Cherchel expedition, October 21, 1942
	3	Darlan, Admiral Jean
	4	Darlan-Boisson-Eisenhower Agreement, December 7, 1942
	5	Darlan-Clark Agreement, November 22, 1942
	6	Europeans in North Africa
	7	French officials in North Africa. Organization charts
	8	Inter-Allied relations

24

46 (Contd.)		ENVOY TO NORTH AFRICA (Contd.)
		Office file, Presidential Envoy and Political Adviser (Contd.)
	9	Miscellany
		North Africa
	10	Economic conditions
	11	Politics and government
	12	Shipping
	13	Supplies
47.	1	North African and French West African Accords
		North African Campaign
	2	Allied invasion
	3	Operation TORCH
	4	Trade
	5	U.S.-French negotiations
	6	United States. Office of Strategic Services (O.S.S.)
	7	Weygand, General Maxime
		Office file, Allied Force Headquarters (AFHQ), French North Africa
	8	Cables, 1942
	9	Correspondence, 1941-1944
	10	Directives, 1942-1943
	11	Finances, 1942-1943
	12	Memoranda, 1943-1944
	13	Press releases, 1943-1944
48.	1-14	Reports
		1942-1943
49.	1-12	1943-1944
50.		Office file as member of American delegation to Allied Conferences. Memoranda, reports, printed material, correspondence, 1943
	1-2	Casablanca Conference, January, 1943
	3	Moscow Conference, October, 1943
	4	Cairo Conference, November, 1943
	5-10	Office file as member of the Allied Advisory Council for Italian and Balkan Affairs. Correspondence, memoranda, reports, 1943-1944
51.		Subject file. Correspondence, memoranda, reports, printed material, 1940-1944
	1-3	Algeria
	4	American missionaries
	5	Americans in North Africa
	6	British in North Africa
	7	British propaganda in France
	8	Clark, Mark
	9	Cole, Felix
	10	Dakar. Map

51 (Contd.)   ENVOY TO NORTH AFRICA (Contd.)
                    Subject file (Contd.)
    11   Europe, 1929-1939
                        France
                            General
    12   Clippings
    13   Map
    14   Radio broadcast - excerpts
    15   Civil affairs
    16   Food supply
    17   German occupation
    18   Naval operations
    19   Politics and government
    20   Franco-Italian Accords
    21   French-German Armistice
    22   French National Committee (Free French)
    23   French propaganda

52. 1   Gaulle, Charles de
     2   Germany. Classified material directive, January
                          11, 1940
     3   Giraud, Henri
     4   Great Britain - Foreign relations - France
     5   Hirsch, Henri L.
     6   Hull, Cordell
     7   Hungary
     8   Hurley, Patrick
     9   Indochina
    10   Italy - Allied Advisory Council
    11   Jews - Repatriation
    12   Kirk, Alexander
    13   Lapeyre, Andre
    14   Lemaigre-Dubreuil, Jacques
    15   Mineral industries
    16   Miranda, Francisco de
    17   Miscellany
    18   Norden, Carl
                      North Africa
    19   Clippings
    20   Maps
    21   Psychological warfare
    22   Roosevelt, Franklin D.
    23   Spain
    24   Stettinius, Edward
    25   U.S.S.R.
                      United States - Foreign relations
    26   General
    27   France
    28   War correspondents
    29   World War I - Peace treaty
                      World War II
    30   General
    31   Allied landings
    32   Postwar planning

		POLITICAL ADVISER, 1944-1949
53.		Correspondence
		General
	1-10	1944-1945
54.	1-11	1945-1946
55.	1-14	1946-1947
56.	1-9	1948-1949
57.	1	Acheson, Dean, 1945-1949
	2	Achilles, Theodore, 1947
	3	Adcock, C.L., 1949
	4	Adenauer, Konrad, 1949
	5	Aldrich, Winthrop, 1945-1948
	6	Allen, George V., 1945-1949
	7	Armour, Norman, 1947
	8	Arnold, Karl, 1949
	9	Aufhauser, Siegfried, 1944-1949
	10	Barrett, Edward W., 1945
	11	Beam, Jacob D., 1947-1950
	12	Bentley, William, 1948
	13	Benton, William, 1947
	14	Berle, Adolf, 1944
	15	Biddle, Francis, 1945-1946
	16	Bird, William, 1945
	17	Bohlen, Charles E., 1946-1947
	18	Brown, Lestrade, 1944-1948
	19	Bullitt, William C., 1948
	20	Butterworth, William W., 1947
	21	Byrnes, James, 1946-1949
	22	Cannon, John K., 1945
	23	Chapin, Selden, 1946
	24	Clark, Mark, 1945-1947
	25	Clay, Lucius, 1947-1949
	26	Clayton, William L., 1944-1947
	27	Cronan, Richard J., 1945
	28	Culbert, F.P., 1948-1949
	29	Davies, Joseph, 1945
	30	DeCourcy, William C., 1946
	31	Donovan, William, 1945-1948
	32	Douglas, Lewis, 1949
	33	Draper, W.H., Jr., 1945-1949
	34	Dulles, Allen, 1944-1948
	35	Dulles, John Foster, 1947-1948
	36	Dunn, James, 1944-1946
	37	Durbrow, Elbridge, 1945
	38	Eisenhower, Dwight D., 1945-1948
	39	Esteva, Georges, 1948
	40	Farley, James, 1945-1949

57 (Contd.)   POLITICAL ADVISER (Contd.)
              Correspondence (Contd.)
    41   Forrestal, James V., 1946-1947
    42   Fullerton, Hugh, 1946

58. 1   Galbraith, John K., 1947
     2   Gellhorn, Martha, 1946-1947
     3   Gerten, Nicholas, 1944-1945
     4   Gibson, Hugh, 1948-1949
     5   Giraud, Henri, 1944
     6   Goethals, Georges, 1946
     7   Gray, Cecil, 1946
     8   Grew, Joseph C., 1944-1945
     9   Gribanov, 1947
    10   Gross, Ernest, 1949
    11   Gruenther, Alfred, 1944-1948
    12   Hardy, Simone, 1948
    13   Harley, F.L., 1944-1945
    14   Harnischfeger, Walter, 1948
    15   Harriman, W. Averell, 1949
    16   Harris, David, 1946
    17   Henry-Haye, Gaston, 1945
    18   Hickerson, John, 1948
    19   Holmes, Julius, 1944-1945
    20   Hoover, Herbert C., 1947-1949
    21   Hopkins, Harry, 1945
    22   Hrones, John, 1946-1949
    23   Hulick, Charles, 1948
    24   Hull, Cordell, 1944-1949
    25   Jacobs, Joseph, 1949
    26   Jessup, Philip, 1948
    27   Jones, J. Wesley, 1945
    28   Kennan, George F., 1947-1948
    29   Keyes, Geoffrey, 1949
    30   King, David, 1947
    31   Knapp, J. Burke, 1949
    32   Krantz, Frederick, 1947
    33   Krantz, Marian, 1947
    34   LaFollette, Charles, 1949
    35   Langer, William, 1947
    36   Laukhuff, Perry, 1949
    37   Leahy, William, 1945-1949
    38   Lemaigre-Dubreuil, Jacques, 1948-1949
    39   LeMay, Curtis, 1948
    40   Likeman, J.L., 1947
    41   Long, Breckinridge, 1944
    42   Lovett, Robert, 1947-1949
    43   Lynch, Robert, 1944-1945
    44   Lyon, Frederick B., 1946
    45   MacArthur, Douglas, II, 1946-1947
    46   MacLeish, Archibald, 1945
    47   Macmillan, Harold, 1944-1947
    48   Magruder, Carter, 1949

58 (Contd.)   POLITICAL ADVISER (Contd.)
                   Correspondence (Contd.)
       49   Marshall, George, 1945-1949
       50   Mast, L., 1945
       51   Matthews, H. Freeman, 1944-1947
       52   McCarthy, Frank, 1945
       53   McCloy, John J., 1949
       54   McGraw, James, 1948-1949
       55   Mefret, Noel, 1945-1949
       56   Merigeault, Rene, 1945
       57   Miao, P.C., 1949
       58   Murphy, Raymond, 1946

59.   1   Nabokoff, Nicolas, 1947
       2   Newman, James, 1948
       3   Nizer, Louis, 1945
       4   North African Economic Board, 1949
       5   O'Brien, William G., 1945-1949
       6   Offie, Carmel, 1944-1949
       7   Oppenheimer, Fritz, 1949
       8   Pasquier, Pierre du, 1946
       9   Patton, George, 1945
       10   Pauley, Edwin W., 1946
       11   Pendar, Kenneth, 1944-1946
       12   Peurifoy, John, 1948-1949
       13   Pinkley, Virgil, 1947
       14   Pollock, James, 1947
       15   Poole, DeWitt, 1946
       16   Pope, Maurice, 1946
       17   Prud'homme, Hector, 1949
       18   Reber, Samuel, 1945-1949
       19   Riddleberger, James, 1946-1949
       20   Roosevelt, Eleanor, 1946
       21   Roosevelt, Franklin D., 1944
       22   Rostow, W.W., 1947
       23   Royall, Kenneth, 1947-1948
       24   Rusk, Dean, 1949
       25   Russell, Donald, 1946
       26   Saint Hardouin, Jacques T. de, 1945-1947
       27   Saltzman, Charles, 1947-1949
       28   Schneider, Douglas, 1945
       29   Sevareid, Eric, 1944
       30   Shaw, G. Howland, 1944
       31   Smith, W. Bedell, 1945
       32   Spellman, Francis Cardinal, 1945-1947
       33   Spofford, Charles, 1946-1947
       34   Steelman, John, 1949
       35   Steingut, Leo, 1944-1945
       36   Stettinius, Edward, Jr., 1944-1946
       37   Stimson, Henry, 1945
       38   Stone, Donald, 1945
       39   Stone, William E., 1948

59 (Contd.) POLITICAL ADVISER (Contd.)
    Correspondence (Contd.)
  40   Strang, William, 1945-1947
  41   Sumner, Edward, 1944-1947
  42   Swope, Herbert Bayard, 1949
  43   Symington, W. Stuart, 1947
  44   Szymczak, M.S., 1947
  45   Taylor, Maxwell, 1948-1949
  46   Truman, Harry, 1945-1947
  47   Tuck, S. Pinkney, 1949
  48   Tully, Grace, 1945
  49   Tuthill, John, 1947-1948
  50   U.S. Department of State, 1945-1949
  51   Vandenberg, Arthur H., 1947
  52   Vaughn, Harry, 1947
  53   Vuillien, Charles, 1946-1949
  54   Vyshinsky, Andrei, 1947
  55   Wallner, Woodruff, 1947
  56   Webb, James E., 1949
  57   Weygand, Jacques, 1946
  58   Wickersham, Neil, 1946

60.   Office file as member of U.S. delegation, Council of
      Foreign Ministers, Moscow, March-April, 1947
  1-2   General
  3   Proceedings
  4   Reports
      Working papers
  5   Coal
  6   Demilitarization
  7   Democratization

61. 1   Denazification
  2   Displaced persons
  3   German assets in Austria
  4   Germany as an economic unit
  5   Inter-Allied Reparations Agency
  6   Limitation of occupation forces
  7   Polish-German frontier

62. 1-2   Preparation of German Peace Treaty
  3   Prisoners of war
  4   Provisional government (of Germany)

63. 1   Reparations
  2   Repatriation of Soviet citizens
  3   Ruhr-Rhineland
  4   Saar

64 (Contd.)		POLITICAL ADVISER, 1944-1949 (Contd.)

64 (Contd.)   POLITICAL ADVISER, 1944-1949 (Contd.)
                    Office file as member of U.S. delegation, Council of
                        Foreign Ministers, Moscow (Contd.)
                            Working papers (Contd.)
    1   Territorial reorganization
    2   Treaty - Disarmament and demilitarization
    3   Trieste
    4   United Nations property in Germany

65.   Office file as member of U.S. delegation, Council of
                        Foreign Ministers, London, November-December, 1947
    1-3   General
                            Working papers
    4   Austria
    5   Economic principles
    6   Germany

66. 1-2   Germany
    3   Peace treaty
    4   Provisional government
    5   Reparations

67.   Office file as member of the U.S. delegation, Council of
                        Foreign Ministers, Paris, May-June, 1949
    1   General
    2-11   Preparatory papers

68.   Working papers
    1   Austria
    2-4   Berlin
    5   Quadripartite draft

69.   Office file as political adviser, Office of the Military
                        Government of the United States (OMGUS)
    1   General
    2   Background information
    3-7   Documents - German government
                                Memoranda, correspondence
                                    Copies of captured German documents,
                                    1938-1943, related to German-Russian
                                    relations, the North African Campaign, and
                                    the conduct of the war; including
                                    agreements and communications between
                                    Russian and German representatives,
                                    communiques from Friedrich von Schulenberg,
                                    Joachim von Ribbentrop, and V.M. Molotov.
                                    Also included are memoranda (in English) to
                                    Robert Murphy describing the documents.
                                    Not all of the documents are complete in
                                    this collection, but are available on
                                    microfilm in the National Archives

69 (Contd.)   POLITICAL ADVISER (Contd.)
              Office file as political adviser, Office of the Military
              Government of the United States (OMGUS) (Contd.)
                  Documents - German government (Contd.)
                      Minutes (incomplete). Meetings of Adolf
                          Hitler and his staff on the conduct of the
                          war, 1942-1945.
    8   Parts 29-34

70. 1   Parts 35-40
    2   Parts 44-53
    3   Reports. Evaluation of the Soviet secret
                          service until the summer of 1944 as
                          observed by the German Front
                          Aufklaerungstruppe III. Report is based on
                          interrogations and captured Russian field
                          orders. English translation entitled,
                          "Organization and Mission of the Soviet
                          Secret Service"
    4-5   Memoranda, including copies of memoranda, 1944-1946

71.   Reports
    1   Agreements on Germany
    2   Certain International and U.S. Policy
                            Documents Regarding Germany
    3   Chronologic Tables on Western Germany, Part I
    4   Chronologic Tables on Western Germany, Part II
    5   Decartelization Program in Germany
    6   Discussion of Possible Constitutional
                            Provisions for a German Federal Government
    7   Documented Chronology on Political
                            Developments Regarding Germany
    8   Documents on German Unity
    9   Economic Prospects of the Russian Zone and
                            Russian Attitude Toward German Unity
    10   History of the Office of Military Government
                            for Germany to 1945

72. 1   International Regimes for Cities
    2   Inter-Zonal Transit Rights and Movement of
                            Forces to Occupation Zones
    3   Military Government Law
    4   Principal Allied Economic Agreements on
                            Germany and Control Agencies
    5   Property Control
    6   Reparations
                        Summary of Multipartite Agreements and
                            Disagreements on Germany
    7   Part I

73. 1   Part II

73. (Contd.)   POLITICAL ADVISER (Contd.)
               Office file as a political adviser, Office of the
                  Military Government of the United States (OMGUS)
                  (Contd.)
                     Reports (Contd.)
     2   Summary of Multipartite Agreements and
                           Disagreements on Germany
     3   Summary of U.S. Statements and Proposals on
                           German Government
     4   U.S. Policy - Germany

74.   Office file as member of U.S. delegation, Tripartite
                  Talks, London, February-April, 1948
     1   General
     2   Memoranda
                   Reports
     3   Benelux
     4   ECA Aid to Bizone
     5   European Recovery Program
     6   German Inventory and Security

75. 1   Germany
    2   Political and Economic Organization
    3   Protection of Allied Interests

76. 1   Reparations
    2   Ruhr
    3   Security
    4   Territorial Arrangement
    5   Trizonia

77.   Subject file. Memoranda, reports, correspondence,
                  printed material, 1944-1949
    1   Allied High Commission for Germany
    2   Allied Military Missions
    3   Baudouin, Paul
    4   Economic cooperation - U.S. and Germany
    5   European Advisory Commission
    6   Field, Noel
    7   Flandin, Pierre
                  France
    8   General, including copies of correspondence
                        between Jesse Straus and Franklin D.
                        Roosevelt
    9   Foreign Legion
   10   Germany - Foreign relations, including copies of
                     minutes of meetings of German leaders;
                     interrogation records
   11   Hitler, Adolf

```
77 (Contd.)     POLITICAL ADVISER (Contd.)
                    Subject file (Contd.)
    12                  Independent League for European Cooperation
    13                  Military Government Conference, August, 1945
    14-15               Miscellany
    16              Union of Soviet Socialist Republics (U.S.S.R.)
                    United States - Foreign relations
    17                  France
    18                  Germany
    19              Voice of America - Russian program

78.             AMBASSADORSHIPS, DEPARTMENT OF STATE, 1949-1959
                    Correspondence
                        General
    1-9                     1950-1952

79. 1-11                    1952-1953

80. 1-12                    1953

81. 1-14                    1953-1954

82. 1-14                    1955

83. 1-14                    1956-1958

84. 1-14                    1958-1959

85. 1-15                    1959

86. 1-16                    1959

87. 1                   Acheson, Alice, 1951
    2                   Acheson, Dean, 1950-1959
    3                   Achilles, Theodore, 1951-1959
    4                   Adams, Ware, 1959
    5                   Aldrich, Winthrop, 1953-1955
    6                   Allen, George, 1956-1959
    7                   Allison, John, 1951-1953
    8                   Alphand, Herve, 1959
    9                   Alverson, Lyle, 1956-1959
    10                  Armour, Norman, 1958-1959
    11                  Armstrong, Clare, 1958
    12                  Arneson, R. Gordon, 1951
    13                  Auchincloss, Hugh, 1953
    14                  Baldridge, H. Malcolm, 1959
    15                  Baldwin, Roger, 1953-1959
    16                  Baruch, Bernard, 1953-1959
    17                  Battle, Lucius, 1949-1959
```

87 (Contd.)   AMBASSADORSHIPS, DEPARTMENT OF STATE (Contd.)
                     Correspondence (Contd.)
       18   Beam, Jacob, 1950-1959
       19   Berenson, Lawrence, 1959
       20   Berle, Adolf, 1952
       21   Bertrand, Henri, 1957-1959
       22   Bess, Demaree, 1954
       23   Bohlen, Charles, 1953
       24   Bond, Niles, 1952
       25   Bonsal, Philip, 1953
       26   Bowie, Robert, 1951
       27   Bradley, Omar, 1950
       28   Briggs, Ellis, 1959
       29   Brockman, H.A., 1958-1959
       30   Brooks, Russell, 1950
       31   Brown, Mr. and Mrs. Irving, 1951-1958
       32   Brown, Lestrade, 1953-1957
       33   Buck, Pearl, 1952
       34   Bullitt, William C., 1950-1957
       35   Burke, Arleigh, 1959
       36   Butz, Earl, 1957-1959
       37   Byers, Clovis, 1959
       38   Byrnes, James, 1950-1959
       39   Byroade, Henry, 1951
       40   Cabot, Thomas, 1951
       41   Capella, Basil, 1953
       42   Carter, Henry, 1951-1959
       43   Chang Chun, 1953
       44   Chiang Kai-shek, 1953
       45   Clark, Mark, 1951-1959
       46   Clay, Lucius, 1950-1958
       47   Corrigan, Robert, 1949-1958
       48   Cowen, Myron, 1953
       49   Cramer, Benjamin, 1953
       50   Cronan, Richard, 1950-1959
       51   Crowe, Philip, 1959
       52   Culbertson, William S., 1953-1954
       53   Cummings, Nathan, 1952-1958
       54   Czapski, Emeric, 1953-1959

88.   1   Darlan, Alain, 1955
        2   Davies, John Paton, 1951
        3   Deak, Francis, 1958-1959
        4   DeCastro, Ralph, 1952-1953
        5   D'Esterno, Mira, 1952-1957
        6   Deverall, Richard, 1953-1959
        7   Dobyns, Thomas G., 1951
        8   Donovan, William, 1952
        9   Doolittle, J.H., 1952

88 (Contd.)   AMBASSADORSHIPS, DEPARTMENT OF STATE (Contd.)
Correspondence (Contd.)

	10	Dooman, Eugene, 1953
	11	Dorn, Frank, 1953
	12	Douglas, Lewis, 1950-1959
	13	Douglas, William O., 1952-1959
	14	Doyle, Albert M., 1950
	15	Draper, William, 1949-1958
	16	Drumright, Everett, 1954
	17	Dulles, Allen, 1951-1959
	18	Dulles, John Foster, 1951-1958
	19	Dunn, James C., 1952-1954
	20	Duranton, Roger, 1952-1954
	21	Durbrow, Elbridge, 1951-1959
	22	Eisenhower, Dwight D., 1951-1958
	23	Eisenhower, Milton, 1954-1957
	24	Elbrick, C. Burke, 1959
	25	Emmerson, John K., 1955
	26	Estes, Thomas, 1959
	27	Fahey, Daniel, 1953
	28	Fairbanks, Douglas, 1949
	29	Farley, James, 1952-1959
	30	Fullerton, Hugh, 1953-1959
	31	Funk, Arthur, 1951-1953
	32	Gibson, Hugh, 1953
	33	Glover, Cato, 1957-1959
	34	Greenwood, E.M., 1957-1958
	35	Grew, Joseph C., 1952-1956
	36	Gross, Ernest A., 1953-1954
	37	Gruenther, Alfred, 1952-1959
89.	1	Hammarskjold, Dag, 1953
	2	Handy, Thomas, 1951
	3	Harrington, Julian, 1953-1955
	4	Henderson, Loy, 1959
	5	Herter, Christian, 1956-1959
	6	Hickerson, John, 1953
	7	Higgins, Frank, 1959
	8	Higgins, Marguerite, 1953-1959
	9	Hillenkoetter, R.H., 1951
	10	Hobby, Oveta Culp, 1953
	11	Hoffman, Paul G., 1954-1956
	12	Hoover, Herbert C., 1955-1959
	13	Hoover, Herbert, Jr., 1957-1959
	14	Hoover, J. Edgar, 1959
	15	Houghton, Amory, 1958-1959
	16	Houghton, Amory, Jr., 1959
	17	Howe, George, 1950
	18	Hull, Cordell, 1950

89 (Contd.)   AMBASSADORSHIPS, DEPARTMENT OF STATE (Contd.)
                     Correspondence (Contd.)

	19	Johnson, U. Alexis, 1953-1959
	20	Johnston, Eric, 1953
	21	Jones, Howard P., 1953-1959
	22	Keeley, James H., 1954
	23	Kennan, George, 1950-1957
	24	Kennedy, John and Jacqueline, 1953-1955
	25	Kennedy, Joseph P., 1953
	26	King, Wunsz, 1952
	27	Kirk, Alexander, 1951
	28	Kocher, Eric, 1953
	29	Kohlberg, Alfred, 1953
	30	Laukhuff, Perry, 1953-1959
	31	Leahy, William, 1950
	32	Lichtenstein, Walter, 1953-1959
	33	Lodge, Henry Cabot, 1953-1959
	34	Lodge, John Davis, 1959
	35	Luce, Clare Boothe, 1954-1959
	36	Lyon, Cecil, 1959
	37	MacArthur, Douglas, II, 1952-1959
	38	Macmillan, Harold, 1949-1959
	39	Mansfield, Mike, 1952-1953
	40	Marshall, George, 1953-1955
	41	Matthews, H. Freeman, 1951-1959
	42	McClelland, Roswell, 1952-1953
	43	McClintock, Robert, 1952-1959
	44	McCloy, John J., 1953-1959
	45	McCormick, Ken, 1950-1953
	46	McGuire, Perkins, 1959
	47	Menuhin, Yehudi, 1949-1959
	48	Merrill, Eugene, 1952-1959
	49	Mesta, Perle, 1952-1955
	50	Middleton, George, 1950
	51	Millard, Hugh, 1951-1954
	52	Morris, Brewster, 1951-1959
	53	Nixon, Richard M., 1956-1959
	54	Norstad, Lauris, 1956
	55	North African Economic Board, 1951-1958
	56	Nuveen, John, 1951-1958
90.	1	O'Brien, William G., 1955-1959
	2	O'Donnell, E.J., 1958-1959
	3	Oestreicher, Sylvan, 1950-1956
	4	Offie, Carmel, 1950-1959
	5	Okazaki, Eimatsu, 1953
	6	Okazaki, Katsuo, 1952-1959
	7	Oppenheimer, Fritz, 1952-1959
	8	Pace, Frank, Jr., 1950-1951

90 (Contd.)   AMBASSADORSHIPS, DEPARTMENT OF STATE (Contd.)
               Correpsondence (Contd.)

	9	Palmer, Ely, 1959
	10	Platzner, Wilfried, 1959
	11	Pogue, Forrest, 1951-1952
	12	Radford, Arthur, 1952-1953
	13	Rankin, Karl, 1953
	14	Raymond, Arthur J., 1951
	15	Reber, Samuel, 1951-1959
	16	Reid, Ogden, 1959
	17	Rhee, Syngman, 1952
	18	Rheinstrom, H., 1956-1959
	19	Riddleberger, James W., 1952-1959
	20	Ridgway, Matthew, 1953-1955
	21	Robertson, Walter, 1953-1959
	22	Rockefeller, John D., III, 1952-1959
	23	Romulo, Carlos, 1959
	24	Roosevelt, Eleanor, 1959
	25	Rose, France de, 1957-1959
	26	Royall, Kenneth, 1949-1959
	27	Rusk, Dean, 1952-1959
	28	Sebald, William J., 1953
	29	Sheean, Vincent, 1959
	30	Skouras, Spyros, 1953-1959
	31	Smith, Bernard, 1958-1959
	32	Smith, W. Bedell, 1950-1955
	33	Spellman, Francis Cardinal, 1951-1959
	34	Stassen, Harold, 1955
	35	Steedman, Alec, 1953
	36	Steeves, John, 1954-1955
	37	Stevens, Robert, 1959
	38	Stevenson, Adlai, 1952
	39	Sulzberger, Arthur H., 1952-1958
	40	Taft, Orray, Jr., 1952-1959
	41	Tanaka, Mitsuo, 1953
	42	Taylor, Maxwell, 1953-1959
	43	Thompson, Tyler, 1953
	44	Tittmann, Harold H., 1954
	45	Tong, Hollington, 1953-1955
	46	Torrente, Henry de, 1955-1959
	47	Truitt, Max, 1951
	48	Truman, Harry, 1952
	49	Voorhees, Tracy, 1950-1953
	50	Wailes, Edward, 1953
	51	Webb, James, 1951
	52	Wedemeyer, Albert C., 1954
	53	Wells, Gladys, 1953-1959
	54	Weygand, Maxime, 1958

91.   AMBASSADORSHIPS, DEPARTMENT OF STATE (Contd.)
              Correspondence (Contd.)
    1   White, Thomas, 1958-1959
    2   Wiley, John C., 1951-1953
    3   Williams, Jack S., 1952-1957
    4   Williams, Margaret, 1952-1958
    5   Williams, Walter, 1959
    6   Willis, Frances, 1955
    7   Wood, John, 1958-1959
    8   Woodward, Robert, 1953-1959
    9   Woodyear, William, 1952-1953
    10   Wright, Jerauld, 1953-1959
    11   Yosano, Shigeru, 1952
    12   Yoshida, Shigeru, 1952-1959
    13   Young, Kenneth, 1953-1958
          Subject file. Printed material, reports, memoranda,
              correspondence, 1949-1959
    14   Eisenhower, Dwight D.
    15   WITHDRAWN. SECURITY CLASSIFIED MATERIAL
    16   Germany
    17   International relations
    18   Israeli-Arab settlement, 1955
    19   Lebanon, 1958
    20   Middle East
    21   Miscellany
    22   Repin, Ilya
    23   Report of the Conference on German External Debts,
                      1952
    24   Russia - History. "The Will of Peter the Great"
    25   United Nations
                  United States
    26   WITHDRAWN. SECURITY CLASSIFIED MATERIAL
    27   Embassy, Belgium

92.   Embassy, Japan
    1-2   Background information
    3   Despatches
    4-5   Entertainment records
    6   Memoranda
    7   Miscellany
    8   Far East Command
                      Foreign relations
    9   General
    10   Japan - Treaties

93.   LATER YEARS, 1959-1978
              Correspondence
                  General
    1   1960
    2   1961
    3   1962

93 (Contd.)   LATER YEARS (Contd.)
                     Correspondence (Contd.)
                         General (Contd.)
         4   1963
         5   1964
         6   1965
         7   1966
         8-9   1967
         10-15   1968

94.   1-15   1968, including correspondence of the
                                       Presidential Transition Committee

95.   1-9   1969, including correspondence of the
                                       Presidential Transition Committee

96.   1-7   1969, including correspondence of the
                                       Presidential Transition Committee (Folder
                                       6 WITHDRAWN. SECURITY CLASSIFIED MATERIAL)
       8-9   1970

97.   1-4   1970
       5-8   1971

98.   1-4   1971
       5-11   1972

99.   1-12   1973

100.   1-5   1974
       6-9   1975
       10-12   1976

101.   1-6   1976
       7-10   1977

102.   1   Abbey, Philip, 1974-1975
       2   Abel, Elie, 1975
       3   Abrams, Creighton W., 1974
       4   Abshire, David, 1970-1976
       5   Acheson, Dean, 1968-1969
       6   Acheson, Alice, 1971
       7   Achilles, Theodore, 1974-1975
       8   Adams, Charles F., 1977
       9   Adenauer, Konrad, 1964
       10   African American Institute, 1970
       11   Agnew, Spiro, 1969
       12   Aldrich, Winthrop W., 1968-1972
       13   Alfalfa Club, 1970-1975
       14   Alibi Club, 1972-1975

102 (Contd.)   LATER YEARS (Contd.)
                Correspondence (Contd.)
        15   All-Language Services, 1975
        16   Allavena, Paul, 1968
        17   Allen, George V., 1968
        18   Allen, Richard V., 1969
        19   Alsop, Stewart, 1973
        20   Altschul, Frank, 1974
        21   Alverson, Lyle T., 1970-1976
        22   Ambach, Dwight R., 1975
        23   American Australian Association, 1970-1971
        24   American Bureau for Medical Aid to China, 1977
        25   American Club of Paris, 1976
        26   American Committee for Assistance to Tunisia, 1973
        27-28   American Council on Germany, 1972-1977
        29   American Federation of Television and Radio
                            Artists, 1969
        30   American Foreign Service Association, 1967-1971
        31   <u>American Foreign Service Journal,</u> 1969
        32   American Heritage Publishing Company, 1968
        33   American Hospital in Paris, 1977
        34   American Irish Historical Society, 1976

103.   1-2   American Korean Foundation, 1972-1976
        3   American Portuguese Society, 1975
        4   American Research Hospital in Poland, 1965-1966
        5   Anderson, George W., Jr., 1969-1975
        6   Annenberg, Walter, 1970-1977
        7   Arai, Yoneo, 1969
        8   Areilza, Jose Ma. de, 1960
        9   Armstrong, Anne, 1973-1976
        10   Armstrong, Hamilton F., 1972
        11   Armstrong, Willis C., 1973-1975
        12   Arrow, Inc., 1972-1973
        13   Asakai, Koichiro, 1963-1977
        14   Asia Society, 1969-1977
        15   Asian Speakers Bureau, 1969
        16   Aspen Institute, 1973
        17   Atlantic Council, 1976
        18   Atlantic Institute, 1968
        19   Avedon, Richard, 1976
        20   Baeder, C. Stewart, 1969-1973
        21   Baer, Elsie, 1975
        22   Baker, William O., 1975
        23   Ball, George W., 1967-1971
        24   Barbour, P., 1976
        25   Barbour, Walworth, 1975-1977
        26   Barnett, A. Doak, 1971-1972

104.   1   Barnett, Frank, 1967-1976
        2   Barr, Joseph, 1968-1969
        3   Barrett, Edward W., 1972-1973

104 (Contd.)   LATER YEARS (Contd.)
              Correspondence (Contd.)
    4   Baruch, Bernard M., Jr., 1974-1977
    5   Bash, Edward J., 1972
    6   Bassin, Jules, 1969
    7   Battle, Lucius D., 1968
    8   Battle, William C., 1969
    9   Battson, Leigh M., 1970
    10   Baudouin, Paul(?), 1960
    11   Beal, John R., 1970-1971
    12   Beam, Jacob D., 1969-1975
    13   Bechtel, Stephen D., 1970
    14   Beichman, Arnold, 1968-1970
    15-16   Belgian American Chamber of Commerce, 1966-1975
    17   Bell, Lawrence G., 1974
    18   Belovsky, Sidney A., 1970
    19   Bendetsen, Karl, 1973
    20   Bennett, Douglas P., 1976
    21   Bennett, Jack F., 1974-1975
    22   Bennett, W. Tapley, Jr., 1969-1977
    23   Berding, Andrew, 1973-1976

105. 1   Berea, George de, 1976
     2   Berenson, Lawrence, 1967-1968
     3   Bergen, John J., 1974-1978
     4   Bergus, Donald C., 1973
     5   Berlin, Isaiah, 1973
     6   Berry, Sidney B., 1975
     7   Bertrand, Henri, 1968-1975
     8   Bess, Dorothy, 1966
     9   Bethouart, Emile, 1975-1977
     10   Bhutto, Zulfikar Ali, 1973
     11   Billemon-Vernaillen, M. et Mme., 1975
     12   Birrenbach, Kurt, 1971-1975
     13   Bishop, Max W.S., 1970-1977
     14   Black, Eugene R., 1967-1971
     15   Blake, James J., 1974-1977
     16   Blake, Robert, 1969-1972
     17   Blomberg, W. Frary von, 1970
     18   Blough, Roger M., 1971
     19   Bohlen, Charles E., 1960-1971
     20   Bourguiba, Habib, 1968-1976
     21   Boyd, John, 1969-1977
     22   Braddock, Daniel M., 1976
     23   Bradley, Gene E., 1973-1974
     24   Braggiotti, D. Chadwick, 1970
     25   Brandt, Willy, 1969
     26   Brennan, William J., Jr., 1969
     27   Briggs, Ellis O., 1968-1971
     28   Briley, John Marshall, 1971
     29   British Broadcasting Company, 1972-1974

105 (Contd.)   LATER YEARS (Contd.)
              Correspondence (Contd.)
    30   Brooks, John, 1973
    31   Broomfield, William S., 1975
    32   Brown, Winthrop, 1971
    33   Bruce, David K.E., 1969-1976
    34   Bruce, James, 1968
    35   Brzezinski, Zbigniew, 1970

106. 1   Buchanan, Wiley T., Jr., 1977
     2   Buckley, William F., Jr., 1967
     3   Bullitt, Orville, 1970-1973
     4   Bullock, Hugh, 1973-1977
     5   Bundy, McGeorge, 1963
     6   Burden, Mr. and Mrs. William, 1969-1975
     7   Burgess, Carter, 1968-1974
     8   Burgess, W. Randolph, 1970-1973
     9   Burke, Arleigh, 1970-1975
    10   Burke, Gerard P., 1976
    11   Burke, James Wakefield, 1969
    12   Burke, Lee H., 1971
    13   Burns, John H., 1969-1971
    14   Burns, Ward, 1970
    15   Bush, Dorothy W., 1972
    16   Bush, George, 1972-1976
    17   Business and Industry Advisory Committee, 1970
    18   Business International Corporation, 1975
    19   Butrick, Richard P., 1971
    20   Butterworth, Mrs. W. Walton, 1975
    21   Butz, Earl L., 1971-1975
    22   Cahill, Kevin, 1974
    23   Calhoun, John A., 1975
    24   Campbell, John F., 1970
    25   Canfield, Cass, 1969
    26   Capehart, Homer, 1962
    27   Carey, Edwin C., 1973
    28   Carey, James J., 1961
    29   Carniero, Maria Cecelia Ribas, 1972
    30   Carpenter, I.W., Jr., 1968
    31   Carter, Jimmy, 1977
    32   Carter, Marshall, 1968
    33   Casey, William J., 1969-1976
    34   Catudal, Honore M., Jr., 1969-1970
    35   Center for Inter-American Relations, 1970-1971
    36   Chambrun, Rene de, 1969-1976
    37   Champion, George, 1968
    38   Chancellor, John, 1973-1974
    39   Chapin, Dwight, 1969
    40   Chapin, Frederick, 1967

107. 1   Chen, Thomas I., 1975-1976
     2   Cherne, Leo, 1969-1977

107 (Contd.)   LATER YEARS (Contd.)
                   Correspondence (Contd.)
         3   Chiang Ching-kuo, 1975
         4   Chiang Kai-shek, Mme. (Soong Mei-ling), 1971
         5   China Institute in America, 1975
         6   Chinese Information Service, 1975
         7   Chow, S.K., 1973
         8   Cicognani, A.G., Cardinal, 1961
         9   Citadel, 1973
        10   Civilian Advisory Panel on Military Manpower
                         Procurement, 1966-1967
        11   Clark, J.J., 1970-1971
        12   Clark, Joan M., 1975
        13   Clark, Mark W., 1967-1974
        14   Clay, Lucius D., 1970-1977
        15   Clemens, Cyril, 1970
        16   Cleveland, Harlan, 1976
        17   Clifford, Clark, 1966-1968
        18   Cline, Ray S., 1976
        19   Clock, Philip, 1968-1972
        20   Close, Mrs. Edward B., 1975
        21   Coburn, John B., 1975
        22   Coffey, Mathew B., 1976
        23   Colby, William E., 1975-1976
        24   Columbia Broadcasting System - CBS News, 1970
        25   Columbia University, 1967-1976
        26   Connally, John B., 1970-1975
        27   Cooke, Terence Cardinal, 1970-1977

108.   1   Cooper, John Sherman, 1968-1973
        2   Cootes, Merritt N., 1972
        3   Corcoran, Thomas G., 1975-1977
        4   Cordier, Andrew W., 1971
        5   Corning Glass Works, 1972
        6   Corrigan, Robert F., 1969-1973
        7   Cors, Allan, 1972
        8   Cort, Stewart S., 1972
        9   Coster, Donald Q., 1969
       10   Council of the Americas, 1972
       11   Council on Foreign Relations, 1962-1971
       12   Craigie, Robert A.P., 1975
       13   Cramer, Robert, 1962
       14   Cronk, Edwin M., 1974
       15   Cross, Cecil M.P., 1973
       16   Csapski, Americ, 1969-1976
       17   Csonka, Emil, 1971
       18   Cummings, Nate, 1960
       19   DACOR (Diplomatic and Consular Officers, Ret.) 1974
       20   Dainelli, Luca, 1971-1977
       21   Dana, William H., 1976
       22   Davies, A. Hudson, 1968

109 (Contd.)   LATER YEARS (Contd.)
              Correspondence (Contd.)
    1   Davies, Rodger P., 1973
    2   Davis, Nathaniel, 1968-1972
    3   Davis, Russell H., Jr., 1970-1973
    4   Davis, Thomas J., III, 1975
    5   Dawson, William, 1964
    6   Dean, Arthur, 1970
    7   DeButts, John D., 1973-1975
    8   Declaration of Atlantic Unity (organization), 1967
    9   Dedijer, S., 1975
   10   DeFreitas, Dick, 1973
   11   Dellisante, Philip, 1975
   12   DeLorenzo, Anthony, 1975
   13   Dennison, Charles S., 1970
   14   Deutch, Michael J., 1971
   15   Dewey, Thomas, 1970
   16   Dickey, Charles D., 1973-1975
   17   Diebold, John, 1971-1975
   18   Dillon, Douglas, 1961
   19   Dombroski, Theresa, 1975
   20   Donaldson, John W., 1973
   21   Donhauser, Robert, 1960
   22   Dorange, General, 1977
   23   Dorschner, John, 1977
   24   Doubleday Corporation, 1971-1974
   25   Douglas, Lewis W., 1971
   26   Douro, Richard, 1967
   27   Dressendorfer, John H., 1969
   28   Ducas, John J., 1970
   29   Dulles, Eleanor Lansing, 1969-1974
   30   Dulles, Mrs. John Foster, 1964
   31   Dunn, James Clement, 1974
   32   Duranton, Roger, 1967-1971
   33   Durbrow, Elbridge, 1971-1976
   34   Durkee, William P., 1974-1975
   35   Eagleburger, Lawrence S., 1975-1976
   36   Eban, Abba, 1967
   37   Eisenhower, David, 1976
   38   Eisenhower, Dwight D., 1960-1961
   39   Eisenhower, John, 1969-1975
   40   Eisenhower, Milton, 1967
   41   Elbrick, C. Burke, 1969
   42   Emmerich, Franz, 1972
   43   Emmet, Christopher, 1967-1973
   44   Engelhard, Jane, 1975
   45   Estes, Thomas S., 1968-1973

110. 1   Fair Campaign Practices Committee, 1975
      2   Fairbanks, Douglas, Jr., 1967
      3   Fales, Rose H., 1974

110 (Contd.) LATER YEARS (Contd.)
                Correspondence (Contd.)

	4	Far East-America Council, 1967-1975
	5	Farland, Joseph S., 1969-1972
	6	Farley, James A., 1963-1975
	7	Fashek, Norman L., 1975
	8	Ferrari, Frank, 1971
	9	Figueroa, Sergio, 1972
	10	Finch, Robert, 1971
	11	Finn, Richard B., 1975
	12	Flanigan, Peter M., 1969
	13	Folger, John Clifford, 1967
	14	Forbes, Malcolm S., 1974
	15	Ford, Gerald, 1968
	16	Ford, Henry, II, 1971
	17	Ford, Thomas, 1970
	18	Foreign Policy Association, 1967-1977
	19	Foreign Reports, 1969-1977
	20	Foreign Service Journal, 1967-1969
	21	Forlani, Arnaldo, 1969-1970
111.	1	Former Members of Congress (organization), 1977
	2	Fortas, Abe, 1968
	3	Fowler, Henry H., 1971-1974
	4	Frankel, Max, 1971
	5	Franklin, William M., 1969-1975
	6	Fredericks, J. Wayne, 1974-1977
	7	Freedom House, 1968
	8	Freeman, Orville L., 1972-1975
	9	Friedrich, Harald, 1968
	10	Friends of Free China, 1973-1974
	11	Fukuda, Takeo, 1969-1975
	12	Fulbright, J. William, 1962
	13	Fullerton, Hugh Stuart, 1967-1976
	14	Funk, Arthur L., 1969-1973
	15	Galbo, Vincent J., 1972
	16	Gallagher, Wes, 1976
	17	Gallman, W.J., 1976
	18	Gandilhon, J., 1968
	19	Gardner, John, 1975
	20	Gardner, Richard, 1973
	21	Garin, Vasco Vieira, 1970
	22	Garner, Robert L., 1968-1972
	23	Garrett, Richard, 1971
	24	Gates, Jack, 1970-1974
	25	Gates, Thomas S., 1976-1977
	26	Gavin, James, 1971
	27	Geliot, Christian, 1967
112.	1-2	George C. Marshall Research Foundation, 1968-1977
	3	George Washington University, 1975-1977

112 (Contd.) LATER YEARS (Contd.)
             Correspondence (Contd.)
    4   Gerhardt, H.A., 1977
    5   German American Chamber of Commerce, 1972
    6   Gilbert, Carl J., 1969
    7   Gilchrist, Andrew and Ella, 1972
    8   Gillan, T.M., 1975
    9   Godley, G. McMurtrie, 1969
   10   Goldberg, Arthur J., 1969
   11   Goldman, Guido, 1974
   12   Goldstern, Norbert, 1969
   13   Goodpaster, A.J., 1968-1977
   14   Gossett, Elizabeth, 1976
   15   Goulli, Slaheddine el, 1972-1975
   16   Gowen, Franklin C., 1975
   17   Grace, J. Peter, 1973
   18   Graham, Robert A., 1976-1977
   19   Green, Marshall, 1971-1974
   20   Greenwood, E.M., 1969-1975
   21   Gromand, Roger, 1975
   22   Gruson, Sydney, 1971
   23   Guiringaud, L. de, 1974
   24   Gutheil, Helmut, 1948-1969

113. 1   Habib, Philip C., 1968-1976
    2   Hagedorn, George C., 1973-1974
    3   Hahn, H.P., 1971
    4   Haider, Michael, 1967
    5   Haig, Alexander, 1970-1972   (SOME ITEMS WITHDRAWN.
                    SECURITY CLASSIFIED MATERIAL)
    6   Haight, G.W., 1968
    7   Halaby, Najeeb E., 1970-1974
    8   Hall, William O., 1972
    9   Halsey, James H., 1975
   10   Handley, William J., 1971
   11   Hanfstaengl, Egon, 1975
   12   Hanser, Richard, 1976
   13   Harder, Howard, 1971
   14   Harlow, Bryce, 1970-1971
   15   Harman, Phillip, 1975-1977
   16   Harriman, W. Averell, 1963-1975
   17   Harrop, William C., 1972
   18   Hartley, Livingston, 1975
   19   Hartwell, Samuel A., 1974
   20   Hauge, Gabriel, 1971-1973
   21   Hays, Brooks, 1976
   22   Heath, Donald R., 1975
   23   Heberle, Jean-Claude, 1971
   24   Heinz, Henry II, 1975
   25   Heiskell, Andrew, 1970
   26   Helms, Richard, 1972-1974

113 (Contd.)   LATER YEARS (Contd.)
                 Correspondence (Contd.)
         27   Henrikson, Alan K., 1976
         28   Henry-Haye, G., 1973-1974
         29   Herter, Christian A., 1961
         30   Herzog, Mrs. Yaacov, 1972
         31   Hesburgh, Theodore M., 1974-1977
         32   Hicks, John F.G., 1967
         33   Hight, John W., 1972
         34   Hill, Robert C., 1969-1973
         35   Hillenbrand, Martin J., 1969
         36   Hinds, A. Boyd, 1972
         37   Hinton, Longstreet, 1975
         38   Hoffman, Mr. and Mrs. Paul G., 1971-1974

114. 1   Hoisington, William A., Jr., 1972
       2   Hoopes, Townsend, 1971-1974
       3   Hoover, Mr. and Mrs. Herbert, Jr., 1967-1969
       4   Hopper, Bruce C., 1967
       5   Horkan, George A., 1967
       6   Hottelet, Richard, 1970
       7   Hotung, Eric, 1970-1973
       8   Houghton, Amory, 1966-1975
       9   Houghton, Arthur A., Jr., 1961-1976
      10   Housman, Richard Jay, 1974
      11   Howley, Frank L., 1969-1970
      12   Hoxie, R. Gordon, 1973
      13   Hoxter, Curtis J., 1971
      14   Hrones, John, 1975
      15   Hsiung, James C., 1977
      16   Hughes, Thomas L., 1968-1969
      17   Humes, John P., 1973
      18   Humphrey, Hubert, 1967
      19   Hunter, Edward, 1975
      20   Ignatieff, Alex, 1974
      21   Ingersoll, Robert S., 1972-1973
      22   Institute of International Education, 1975-1977
      23   International Executive Service Corps, 1967
      24   International Management and Development Institute,
                       1972-1975

115. 1-6   International Rescue Committee, 1969-1977
       7   International Telephone and Telegraph Company, 1973
       8   Irvine, Reed J., 1969
       9   Irwin, John, 1969-1973
      10   Jackson, Henry M., 1967-1969
      11   Janeway, Eliot, 1971
      12   Japan America Institute, 1972
      13   Japan American Cultural Society, 1975

116.   LATER YEARS (Contd.)
              Correspondence (Contd.)
  1   Japan Fund, 1972
  2   Japan International Christian University
                        Foundation, 1973-1977
  3   Japan National Student Association, 1969-1975
  4   Japan Society, 1969-1975
  5   Johari, Gyan, 1969
  6   Johnson, Lyndon B., 1968
  7   Johnson, Mrs. Lyndon B., 1968
  8   Johnson, U. Alexis, 1968-1976
  9   Jones, Harry W., 1976
  10   Jones, James, 1970
  11   Jones, Roger W., 1961
  12   Jousse, General, 1973-1975
  13   Judd, Walter H., 1972
  14   Kaspi, Andre, 1972
  15   Kearns, Henry, 1971
  16   Keating, Kenneth, 1969
  17   Kelly, John E., 1970
  18   Kelsey, John W., Jr., 1969
  19   Kennan, George, 1977
  20   Kennedy, Edward M., 1977
  21   Kennedy, John F., 1960
  22   Kennedy, Mrs. Joseph, 1969
  23   Kennedy, Robert F., 1966-1967
  24   Kern, Harry F., 1968-1977
  25   Kerr, Walter, 1971
  26   Kessler, Frank, 1976
  27   Khan, Najmul Saqib, 1972-1975
  28   Kim, Young Sun, 1972
  29   Kissinger, Henry, 1970-1975   (SOME MATERIAL
                        WITHDRAWN. SECURITY CLASSIFIED MATERIAL)

117. 1   Klein, Julius, 1968-1972
     2   Kline, Hugh, 1975
     3   Knapp, J. Burke, 1975
     4   Knight, Ridgway B., 1969
     5   Knoppers, Antonie T., 1975
     6   Knowlton, William A., 1974
     7   Knox, John, 1972
     8   Knox, William, 1967
     9   Koehler, John O., 1972
     10   Kohler, Foy D., 1967-1976
     11   Kolko, Gabriel, 1969
     12   Korry, Edward M., 1975
     13   Koubbi, Albert el, 1974-1977
     14   Kraus, Maria, 1964-1965
     15   Krock, Arthur, 1966
     16   Kuhn, Irene Corbally, 1967-1975
     17   Kupferman, Theodore, 1968

117 (Contd.)   LATER YEARS (Contd.)
              Correspondence (Contd.)
       18   LaFollette, Charles D., 1967-1971
       19   Laird, Melvin R., 1973
       20   Lamont, Thomas S., n.d.
       21   Land, Edwin H., 1970
       22   Langer, William, 1969
       23   Lasky, Melvin J., 1971
       24   Latimer, Thomas K., 1975
       25   Launay, J.F. de, 1969
       26   Lazrus, Oscar M., 1976
       27   League of Americans Residing Abroad, 1967
       28   Lehaney, Francis, 1971-1975
       29   Lehmann, Manfred R., 1976
       30   Lemaigre-Dubreuil, Jean-Pierre, 1974-1975
       31   Lemnitzer, L.L., 1960
       32   Leonard, Richard G., 1971
       33   Leonhart, William, 1969-1974
       34   Levy-Despas, Andre, 1961
       35   Lewis, Joseph, 1975
       36   Li, K.T., 1973
       37   Li, Mo, 1975-1976
       38   Library of Presidential Papers, 1967-1968
       39   Lilienthal, David E., 1969

118.   1   Lindsay, Franklin A., 1971
        2   Lindsay, John V., 1973
        3   Lodge, Henry Cabot, 1958-1974
        4   Lodge, John Davis, 1960-1972
        5   Lodigensky, A.A., 1971
        6   Loeb, John L., 1975
        7   Loh, I-Cheng, 1971-1977
        8   Longworth, Mrs. Nicholas, 1974
        9   Loridan, Walter, 1969
       10   Loughran, Jack, 1976-1977
       11   Lovestone, Jay, 1967-1971
       12   Lovett, Robert A., 1970
       13   Lowenthal, Abraham F., 1975
       14   Lubbers, Arend P., 1973-1976
       15   Luce, Clare Boothe, 1975
       16   Luce, Henry, III, 1973
       17   Ludden, Raymond, 1969
       18   Lynch, R.J., 1971
       19   Lyon, Cecil B., 1967-1977
       20   MacArthur, Douglas, II, 1970-1971
       21   MacAvoy, Thomas C., 1975
       22   Macmillan, Harold, 1967-1973
       23   Macomber, William B., Jr., 1969-1971
       24   Mahoney, James P., 1972
       25   Maillard, William S., 1974
       26   Manning, Bayliss, 1975-1977

118 (Contd.) LATER YEARS (Contd.)
Correspondence (Contd.)

	27	Mansfield, Mike, 1976-1977
	28	Marcos, Imelda, 1974
	29	Marie Salvatora, Sister, 1975
	30	Marquette University, 1971-1977
	31	Martin, Graham A., 1968
	32	Martin, William McC., Jr., 1969
	33	Marwell, David G., 1977
	34	Mast, Charles, 1970-1977
	35	Mathias, Charles Mc., Jr., 1967-1975
	36	May, Dick, 1967
	37	Mayer, Charles T., 1963-1977
	38	McBride, Robert, 1968-1969
	39	McCarthy, Frank, 1970
	40	McChrystal, Arthur J., 1976-1977
	41	McClintock, Robert, 1968-1973
	42	McCloy, John J., II, 1971-1977
119.	1	McCone, John A., 1961-1971
	2	McCormick, Ken, 1967-1969
	3	McDowell, Robert H., 1969
	4	McFall, Jack K., 1977
	5	McFarland, Joseph B., 1974
	6	McGhee, George C., 1965-1977
	7	McGregor, Robert G., 1969
	8	McIlvaine, Robinson, 1972
	9	McIntyre, J.M., 1960
	10	McMahon, William, 1970
	11	McNamara, Robert S., 1975
	12	Meany, George, 1969-1975
	13	Mefret, Noel, 1969-1971
	14	Melandri, Pierre, 1974
	15	Melbourne, Roy M., 1971
	16	Menuhin, Moshe, 1971
	17	Menuhin, Yehudi, 1968-1976
	18	Menzies, Robert G., 1972
	19	Merchant, Livingston, 1960-1967
	20	Meyer, Armin, 1969-1971
	21	Meyer, Charles A., 1972-1973
	22	Meyer, Frank, 1969
	23	Meyer, John M., Jr., 1970-1976
	24	Middendorf, J. William, II, 1969-1975
	25	Milburn, Bryan, 1967
	26	Miller, Gething C., 1971
	27	Millington-Drake, Eugen, 1972
	28	Moellering, John H., 1974
	29	Mommsen, Ernst Wolf, 1972
	30	Monnet, Jean, 1975-1977
	31	Moore, John D.J., 1969

119 (Contd.) LATER YEARS (Contd.)
                Correspondence (Contd.)
    32   Moore, Walden, 1970-1971
    33   Moorer, Thomas H., 1971-1975
    34   Morgan Guaranty Trust Company, 1969-1975

120. 1   Moro, Aldo, 1969
     2   Mountbatten, The Earl of, 1970
     3   Moynihan, Daniel P., 1976
     4   Mulligan, Dennis J., 1969-1974
     5   Mundt, Karl E., 1968
     6   Murphy, Charles J.V., 1969
     7   Murphy, Gavin, 1977
     8   Murphy, Richard W., 1974
     9   Murphy, Robert D., Jr., 1970
    10   Murphy, Thomas A., 1975
    11   Nagorski, Zygmunt, 1975
    12   Nakashima, Nobuyuki, 1975-1977
    13   Nakasone, Yasuhiro, 1973
    14   Nara, Yasuhiko, 1967-1969
    15   National Association of Manufacturers, 1967-1975
    16   National Conference of Christians and Jews,
                        1972-1976
    17   National Foreign Trade Council, 1969
    18   National Planning Association, 1970
    19   Neff, John C., 1967
    20   Nehru, B.K., 1967
    21   Nelson, Walter Henry, 1970
    22   Newsom, David D., 1972
    23   Newton, Henry, 1969
    24   Nitze, Paul H., 1974
    25   Nixon, Patricia, 1969-1971
    26   Nixon, Richard M., 1967-1976
    27   Norden, Carl F., 1967
    28   Norris, Robert B., 1971
    29   Norstad, Lauris, 1971
    30   O'Brien, John A., 1973
    31   O'Brien, William, 1970-1976
    32   O'Connor, Roderic, 1972
    33   Oehlert, B.H., Jr., 1970
    34   Oestreicher, Sylvan, 1970-1972
    35   Offie, Carmel, 1967-1971
    36   Onassis, Aristotle, 1973
    37   Oppenheimer, Franz M., 1967-1968
    38   Osborn, David, 1973
    39   Overby, Andrew N., 1967-1971
    40   Ovidio, Antonio d', 1969

121. 1   Packard, David, 1977
     2   Packer, Earl L., 1975
     3   Paley, William S., 1975

121 (Contd.) LATER YEARS (Contd.)
              Correspondence (Contd.)
       4   Paris American Club, 1968
       5   Parks, Robert B., 1967
       6   Parsons, Jeanne, 1973
       7   Pasquet, Mme. Maurice, 1975
       8   Pasquier, Pierre du, 1967-1969
       9   Pasquier, Verena du, 1976
      10   Pauphilet, B., 1968-1969
      11   Peale, Norman Vincent, 1975
      12   Pearson, Lester, 1967
      13   Pedersen, Richard F., 1971-1975
      14   Perkins, Richard, 1975
      15   Peterfi, William O., 1972
      16   Petersen, Howard C., 1975
      17   Petree, Virginia H., 1974-1975
      18   Petrov, Vladimir, 1969
      19   Philpott, Robert J., 1976
      20   Phleger, Herman, 1972-1975
      21   Picot, Willy George, 1972
      22   Pinay, Antoine, 1973
      23   Pinkley, Virgil, 1970-1972
      24   Plaza, Galo, 1970
      25   Plimpton, Francis T.P., 1971-1975
      26   Plitt, James R., 1970-1976
      27   Polk, Mrs. Judd N., 1975
      28   Popper, David H., 1969
      29   Porter, Dwight J., 1970
      30   Porter, William J., 1971-1974
      31   Potter, Gary, 1967
      32   Prochnow, Herbert V., 1971
      33   Protter, Benjamin, 1968-1975
      34   Rabb, Maxwell M., 1967
      35   Rabin, Yitzhak, 1970
      36   Radford, Arthur W., 1970
      37   Radvanyi, Janos, 1970
      38   Raghavan, Jai D., 1975

122.   1   Ramsbotham, Peter, 1975
       2   Ramsey, James, 1971
       3   Read, Benjamin H., 1969
       4   Rees, David, 1969
       5   Reid, W. Stafford, 1970
       6   Reischauer, Edwin O. and Haru, 1961-1977
       7   Republican National Committee, 1967
       8   Reston, James, 1970
       9   Ribicoff, Abraham, 1975-1976
      10   Rice, Louis J., Jr., 1975
      11   Richardson, Elliot L., 1969-1975
      12   Riddleberger, James W., 1962-1969
      13   Ridgway, Matthew B., 1971-1976

122 (Contd.) LATER YEARS (Contd.)
       Correspondence (Contd.)
  14   Riess, Curt, 1976
  15   Roach, Perry, 1975-1977
  16   Roche, James M., 1970-1976
  17   Rockefeller, David, 1970-1977
  18   Rockefeller, James S., 1967
  19   Rockefeller, John D., III, 1967-1975
  20   Rockefeller, Mr. and Mrs. Nelson A., 1974-1977
  21   Rockefeller Public Service Awards, 1967-1973
  22   Rockwell, Stuart W., 1970-1973
  23   Rogers, William P., 1970-1972
  24   <u>Rolling Stone,</u> 1976
  25   Romney, George, 1967
  26   Romney Associates, 1967
  27   Romulo, Carlos, 1972-1974
  28   Rooney, Catherine, 1975
  29   Rooney, John J., 1970-1974
  30   Rosenberg, Elliot, 1973
  31   Rositzke, Harry, 1975
  32   Rostow, Eugene V., 1970-1976
  33   Rostow, Walt W., 1969-1970
  34   Roudakoff, Paul, 1976
  35   Rountree, William M., 1972-1973
  36   Rowan, Leslie, 1967
  37   Rowney, E., 1977
  38   Rubloff, Arthur, 1971-1977
  39   Rubottom, R. Richard, Jr., 1967-1969
  40   Rueff, Jacques, 1975
  41   Rueger, William F., 1977
  42   Rumsfeld, Donald H., 1975
  43   Rush, Kenneth, 1974-1977
  44   Rusk, Dean, 1960-1975
  45   Russell, Mrs. Irving, 1974-1975
  46   Rutledge, Campbell, Jr., 1967-1977

123. 1   Saccio, Leonard J., 1970
  2   Safire, William, 1977
  3   Saltonstall, Leverett, 1966
  4   Saltzman, Charles E., 1973-1977
  5   Samuels, Nathaniel, 1972-1974
  6   Sandusky, Michael C., 1976
  7   Sarnoff, Robert W., 1967-1975
  8   Sato, Eisaku, 1967-1969
  9   Satterthwaite, Joseph C., 1975
  10   Sause, Mrs. Oliver, 1975
  11   Scali, John A., 1973
  12   Schaefer, Steve, 1975
  13   Scheuer, Sidney H., 1970
  14   Schlesinger, James R., 1971-1975
  15   Schmidt, Helmut, 1971-1974

123 (Contd.) LATER YEARS (Contd.)
                Correspondence (Contd.)

	16	Scott, Hugh, 1967-1975
	17	Scott, John, 1970-1976
	18	Scranton, William M., 1976
	19	Scribner, Fred C., Jr., 1961
	20	Seaborg, Glenn T., 1971
	21	Searle, William A., 1970-1973
	22	Seeds, Robert, 1974
	23	Seignious, George M., II, 1974
	24	Senoussi, Badreddine, 1973
	25	Shah, Konsin C., 1975-1977
	26	Shaine, H.B., 1973
	27	Sheean, Mrs. Vincent, 1975
	28	Sheehan, John E., 1972
	29	Shepley, James R., 1975
	30	Shoji, Keijiro, 1971
	31	Shriver, R. Sargent, Jr., 1968
	32	Shultz, George, 1972-1974
	33	Simon, Eugene, 1975-1977
	34	Simon, William E., 1974
	35	Singer, Herbert, 1967
	36	Sisco, Joseph J., 1971-1974
	37	Smalley, Walter, 1967
	38	Smith, Carleton, 1969
	39	Smith, Gerard C., 1971-1974
	40	Smith, James S., 1975
	41	Smith, Richard J., 1976
	42	Smith, Richard W., 1976
	43	Sneider, Richard L., 1972
	44	Societe Anonyme Belge D'Exploitation de la Navigation Aerienne (SABENA), 1969
	45	Soffer, Elie, 1967-1973
	46	Soustelle, Jacques, 1975
	47	Spellman, Francis Cardinal, 1964
	48	Spivak, Lawrence, 1975
	49	Springer, Axel, 1971-1972
	50	Stabler, Wells, 1974
	51	Staercke, Andre de, 1969
	52	Standish, Myles, 1975
124.	1	Stans, Maurice, 1969-1970
	2	Stanton, Frank, 1972-1975
	3	Steedman, Alec, 1960-1976
	4	Steeves, John M., 1967-1970
	5	Stegmaier, John L., 1971
	6	Stephens, John W., 1969
	7	Stevens, Robert, 1971-1977
	8	Stoessel, Walter, 1968
	9	Stone, Galen L., 1975
	10	Straus, Oscar S., II, 1969-1972

124 (Contd.)   LATER YEARS (Contd.)
                   Correspondence (Contd.)
        11   Straus, Ralph I., 1972-1976
        12   Strauss, Lewis L., 1969-1971
        13   Strausz-Hupe, Robert, 1967-1972
        14   Struelens, Michel, 1976
        15   Sugahara, K., 1970-1971
        16   Sullivan, Joseph T.P., 1972-1977
        17   Sulzberger, Arthur Ochs, 1974
        18   Sun Yun-suan, 1974-1977
        19   Surrey Probation Area, 1961
        20   Symington, W. Stuart, 1969-1975
        21   Taft, Philip, 1972
        22   Tanguy, Charles R., 1969-1972
        23   Tasca, Henry, 1971-1975
        24   Teissier, Jacques, 1973-1977
        25   Tello, Manuel, 1964
        26   Thai, Nguyen, 1969
        27   Thompson, Mr. and Mrs. Llewellyn, 1967-1977
        28   Togo, Fumihiko, 1977
        29   Tomabechi, T., 1975

125. 1   Torres, Baron de las, 1960
        2   Tournaire, J.A., 1975
        3   Trebesch, Herbert, 1969
        4   Tresize, Philip, 1969
        5   Trilateral Commission, 1975
        6   Trowbridge, A.B., 1967
        7   Turner, Stansfield, 1977
        8   Turner, William C., 1976
        9   Tute, Warren, 1976
        10   Tuthill, John W., 1970-1974
        11   Twining, Nathan, 1960
        12   Twitchell, Kenaston, 1967-1975
        13   Ungerer, Werner, 1976
        14   United Nations Association of the United States of
                          America, 1969-1970
        15   United States Council, 1975
        16   United States Council of the International Chamber
                          of Commerce, 1967
        17   United States Korea Economic Council, 1975
        18   United States Mission to the United Nations, 1975
        19   University Club, 1969-1976
        20   Upston, John E., 1968-1975
        21   Ushiba, Nobuhiko, 1971-1973
        22   Vailati, Vanna, 1966
        23   Vance, Cyrus, 1976-1977
        24   Vernon, Raymond, 1974-1976
        25   Veterans of Foreign Wars, 1972-1975
        26   Volcker, Paul A., 1975

126.   LATER YEARS (Contd.)
                 Correspondence (Contd.)
      1   Wallin, Paul J., 1973
      2   Walmsley, Walter N., 1960
      3   Watson, Thomas J., Jr., n.d.
      4   Watts, W. Walter, 1967
      5   Watts, William, 1977
      6   Waugh, Samuel C., 1961
      7   Webb, James E., 1968
      8   Wedemeyer, A.C., 1970
      9   Weinstein, Martin E., 1968
      10   Weisbrod, Ray, 1961
      11   Weyl, Nathaniel, 1967
      12   Whitcomb, Philip W., 1969-1977
      13   Whitehouse, Charles S., 1975
      14   Whitman, Ann C., 1961-1975
      15   Wiley, Alexander, 1960
      16   Woods, Rose Mary, 1969-1972
      17   Wright, Jerauld, 1969-1977
      18   Wriston, Henry, 1967-1975
      19   Wyden, Peter H., 1970
      20   Wyman, Thomas H., 1970
      21   Yamazaki, Toshio, 1974
      22   Yasukawa, Takeshi, 1973-1976
      23   Yeh, George, 1973
      24   Yen, C.K., 1975
      25   Yost, Charles W., 1970
      26   Young, R.A., 1970
      27   Zablocki, Clement J., 1976-1977
      28   Zahedi, Ardeshir, 1973-1974
      29   Zahn, Joachim, 1970-1976
      30   Zakaria, H.M.A., 1974
      31   Zanuck, Darryl F., 1970
      32   Zayas, Alfred M. de, 1976-1977
      33   Zorlu, Fatin Rusto, 1960
      34   Zurhellen, J. Owen, Jr., 1975-1977

127.   Office file as member of the Commission on the
                 Organization of the Government for the Conduct of
                 Foreign Policy
                    General
      1-7   March-November, 1973

128. 1-6   November-December, 1973

129. 1-7   January-June, 1974

130. 1-11   July-December, 1974

131. 1-12   January-June, 1975

132. 1   Summaries of testimony, June, 1973 -
                             September, 1974

133.   LATER YEARS (Contd.)
              Office file as member of the Commission on the
                Organization of the Government for the Conduct of
                Foreign Policy (Contd.)
     1-5   Printed report, Appendices, volumes 1-4

134. 1-3   Appendices, volumes 5-7

135.   Subject file. Printed material, memoranda,
                    correspondence, and reports, 1959-1978
     1   American Embassy, Bern, Switzerland
     2   American Freedom from Hunger Foundation
     3   American Institute for Free Labor Development
     4   Association Internationale des Etudiants en
                      Sciences Economiques et Commerciales
     5-6   Association de la Liberation Francaise du 8
                      Novembre 1942
     7   Atlantic Council
     8   Baker, William O.
     9   Behm, Douglas
     10   Bennett, W. Tapley, Jr.
     11   Berlin
     12-14   Bilderberg Group

136. 1-15   Bilderberg Group

137. 1-2   Bilderberg Group
     3   Bishop, Max W.
     4   Brookings Institution Seminar, November 12, 1975
     5   Bullitt, William C.
     6   Carter, Jimmy
     7   Catholic Church Encyclical
     8   Center for the Study of the Presidency
     9   Chiang Kai-shek
     10-13   China
     14   Citadel
     15   Clay, Lucius D.

138. 1-2   Council on Foreign Relations
     3   Dominican Republic
     4   Eisenhower, Dwight D.
     5   Far East-America Council
     6   France-America Society
     7   Fund for Peace
     8   Geopolitics
     9   George C. Marshall Research Foundation
     10   Goldwater, Barry
     11   Greece
     12   Gruber, Karl
     13   Houghton, Amory

138 (Contd.)		LATER YEARS (Contd.)
		Subject file (Contd.)
	14	Intelligence service
	15	International economic relations
	16	International Executive Service Corps
	17	Italy
139.	1	Japan - Economic conditions
	2	Japan Fund
	3-4	Japan Society
	5	Johnson, Lyndon B.
	6	Jolly, Edwin J.
	7	Lamont, Thomas
	8	Marshall Plan
	9	Mesta, Perle
	10-11	Miscellany
	12	Morgan Guaranty Trust Company
140.	1-6	National Conference of Christians and Jews
	7-8	National Export Expansion Council
	9	National Planning Association
	10	North African Economic Board
141.	1-8	Pakistan Cyclone Relief Fund
	9-10	Project Hope
142.	1-3	Project Hope
	4	Public Advisory Committee for Trade Negotiations
	5-15	Radio Free Europe
143.	1	Searle, William A.
	2	Tordella, Dr. (Nominee for Rockefeller Award)
	3	United Nations Association of the United States of America
		United States
	4-5	Department of State
	6	Economic conditions
	7	Foreign relations
	8	United States Committee for Refugees
	9-12	United States Council of the International Chamber of Commerce
	13	United States Overseas Information and Cultural Program
	14	Wang Li-yen
	15	World Rehabilitation Fund
	16	World Trade Fair, Yugoslavia, September 10-12, 1970
144.		OVERSIZE FILE, 1943-1967
		6 albums of clippings, 1949-1951; 1 photograph album, Florennes, Belgium, 1951; 3 certificates commemorating appointments to the Foreign Intelligence Advisory Board, 1961 and 1965, and the National Export Expansion Council, 1967

145.	OVERSIZE FILE (Contd.) Flag
146.	Olive branch from tree under which Italian armistice was signed, September, 1943 Original of cartoon Algerian talisman, July, 1944 Engraved desk set

PHONOTAPES

Tapes 1-3	Notre Dame University meeting, April 13, 1959 (3 reels)
Tapes 4-5	Luncheon for Under Secretary of State Robert Murphy, ca. 1959 (2 reels)
Env. A-000	PHOTOGRAPHS. 1,298 personal and official photographs. A detailed listing exists in the Photo Card Catalog in the Hoover Institution Archives reading room.

INDEX

Entry numbers refer to page numbers.

Abbey, Philip	39
Abel, Elie	39
Abrams, Creighton W.	39
Abshire, David	39
Acheson, Alice	33, 39
Acheson, Dean	18, 26, 33, 39
Achilles, Theodore	26, 33, 39
Adams, Charles F.	39
Adams, Ware	33
Adcock, C.L.	26
Adenauer, Konrad	10, 26, 39
African American Institute	39
Agnew, Spiro	39
Akihito, Prince	16
Aldrich, Winthrop W.	26, 33, 39
Alfalfa Club	39
Algeria	24
Alibi Club	39
All-Language Services	40
Allavena, Paul	40
Allen, George V.	26, 33, 40
Allen, Richard V.	40
Allied Advisory Council for Italian and Balkan Affairs	24
Allied Force Headquarters	24
Allied High Commission for Germany	32
Allied Military Missions	32
Allied operations, December 1941-July, 1942	23
Allison, John	33
Alphand, Herve	33
Alsop, Stewart	40
Altschul, Frank	40
Alverson, Lyle T.	22, 33, 40
Ambach, Dwight R.	40
American Australian Association	40
American Bureau for Medical Aid to China	40
American Club of Paris	40
American Committee for Assistance to Tunisia	40
American Council on Germany	40
American Embassy, Bern, Switzerland	57
American Federation of Television and Radio Artists	40
American Foreign Service Association	40
American Foreign Service Journal	40
American Freedom from Hunger Foundation	57
American Heritage Publishing Company	40
American Hospital in Paris	40
American Institute for Free Labor Development	57
American Irish Historical Society	40
American Korean Foundation	40
American missionaries	24
American Portuguese Society	40

American Research Hospital in Poland 40
Americans in North Africa 24
Anderson, George W., Jr. 40
Annenberg, Walter 40
Anslinger, H.J. 22
Arai, Yoneo 40
Areilza, Jose Ma. de 40
Armour, Norman 26, 33
Armstrong, Anne 40
Armstrong, Clare 33
Armstrong, Hamilton F. 40
Armstrong, Willis C. 40
Arneson, R. Gordon 33
Arnold, Karl 26
Arrow, Inc. 40
Asakai, Koichiro 40
Asia Society 40
Asian Speakers Bureau 40
Aspen Institute 40
Association de la Liberation Francaise du 8 Novembre 1942 57
Association Internationale des Etudiants en Sciences Economiques et
    Commerciales 57
Atlantic Council 40, 57
Atlantic Institute 40
Auchincloss, Hugh 33
Aufhauser, Siegfried 26
Austria 30
Avedon, Richard 40
Baeder, C. Stewart 40
Baer, Elsie 40
Baker, William O. 40, 57
Baldridge, H. Malcolm 33
Baldwin, Roger 33
Ball, George W. 40
Barbour, P. 40
Barbour, Walworth 40
Barnett, A. Doak 40
Barnett, Frank 40
Barr, Joseph 40
Barrett, Edward W. 26, 40
Baruch, Bernard 33
Baruch, Bernard M., Jr. 22, 41
Bash, Edward J. 41
Bassin, Jules 41
Battle, Lucius D. 33, 41
Battle, William C. 41
Battson, Leigh M. 41
Baudouin, Paul 32, 41
Bavaria 21
Beal, John R. 19, 41
Beam, Jacob D. 26, 34, 41

Bechtel, Stephen D. 41
Behm, Douglas 57
Beichman, Arnold 41
Belgian American Chamber of Commerce 41
Bell, Lawrence G. 41
Belovsky, Sidney A. 41
Bendetsen, Karl 41
Bennett, Douglas P. 41
Bennett, Jack F. 41
Bennett, W. Tapley, Jr. 41, 57
Bentley, William 26
Benton, William 26
Berding, Andrew 41
Berea, George de 41
Berenson, Lawrence 34, 41
Bergen, John J. 41
Bergus, Donald C. 41
Berle, Adolf 26, 34
Berlin 30, 57
Berlin, Isaiah 41
Bernstein, Philip S. 19
Berry, Sidney B. 41
Bertrand, Henri 34, 41
Bertrand-Vigne, Georges 22
Bess, Demaree 34
Bess, Dorothy 41
Bethouart, Emile 41
Bhutto, Zulfikar Ali 41
Biddle, Francis 26
Bilderberg Group 57
Billemon-Vernaillen, M. et Mme. 41
Bird, William 26
Birrenbach, Kurt 41
Bishop, Max W.S. 41, 57
Black, Eugene R. 41
Blake, James J. 41
Blake, Robert 41
Blomberg, W. Frary von 41
Blough, Roger M. 41
Bohlen, Charles E. 26, 34, 41
Boisson, Pierre 22
Bond, Niles 34
Bonsal, Philip 34
Bourguiba, Habib 41
Bowie, Robert 34
Boyd, John 41
Braddock, Daniel M. 41
Bradley, Gene E. 41
Bradley, Omar 34
Braggiotti, D. Chadwick 41
Brandt, Willy 41
Brennan, William J., Jr. 41
Brewster, Ralph O. 22

```
Briggs, Ellis O. .................................................34, 41
Briley, John Marshall ...............................................41
British Broadcasting Company ........................................41
British in North Africa .............................................24
British propaganda in France ........................................24
Brockman, H.A. ......................................................34
Brookings Institution ...............................................57
Brooks, John ........................................................42
Brooks, Russell .....................................................34
Broomfield, William S. ..............................................42
Brown, Lestrade .............................................22, 26, 34
Brown, Mr. and Mrs. Irving ..........................................34
Brown, Winthrop .....................................................42
Bruce, David K.E. ...................................................42
Bruce, James ........................................................42
Brzezinski, Zbigniew ................................................42
Buchanan, Wiley T., Jr. .............................................42
Buck, Pearl .........................................................34
Buckley, William F., Jr. ............................................42
Bullitt, Orville ....................................................42
Bullitt, William C. .....................................22, 26, 34, 57
Bullock, Hugh .......................................................42
Bundy, McGeorge .....................................................42
Burden, Mr. and Mrs. William ........................................42
Burgess, Carter .....................................................42
Burgess, W. Randolph ................................................42
Burke, Arleigh ..................................................34, 42
Burke, Gerard P. ....................................................42
Burke, James Wakefield ..............................................42
Burke, Lee H. .......................................................42
Burns, John H. ......................................................42
Burns, Ward .........................................................42
Bush, Dorothy W. ....................................................42
Bush, George ........................................................42
Business and Industry Advisory Committee ............................42
Business International Corporation ..................................42
Butrick, Richard P. .................................................42
Butterworth, Mrs. W. Walton .........................................42
Butterworth, William W. .............................................26
Butz, Earl L. ...................................................34, 42
Byers, Clovis .......................................................34
Byrnes, James ...................................................26, 34
Byroade, Henry ......................................................34
Cabot, Thomas .......................................................34
Caffrey, Jefferson ..................................................10
Cahill, Kevin .......................................................42
Cairo Conference, November, 1943 ....................................24
Calhoun, John A. ....................................................42
Campbell, John F. ...................................................42
Canfield, Cass ......................................................42
Cannon, John K. .....................................................26
Capehart, Homer .....................................................42
Capella, Basil ......................................................34
```

Carey, Edwin C. 42
Carey, James J. 42
Carniero, Maria Cecelia Ribas 42
Carpenter, I.W., Jr. 42
Carr, Wilbur 21
Carter, Henry 34
Carter, Jimmy 42, 57
Carter, Marshall 42
Casablanca Conference, January, 1943 24
Casey, William J. 42
Catholic Church Encyclical 57
Catudal, Honore M., Jr. 42
Center for Inter-American Relations 42
Center for the Study of the Presidency 57
Chambrun, Rene de 42
Champion, George 42
Chancellor, John 42
Chang Chun 34
Chapin, Dwight 42
Chapin, Frederick 42
Chapin, Mrs. James P. 22
Chapin, Selden 26
Chen, Thomas I. 42
Cherchel expedition, October 21, 1942 23
Cherne, Leo 42
Cherrington, Edwin 21
Chiang Ching-kuo 43
Chiang Kai-shek 20, 34, 57
Chiang Kai-shek, Mme. 43
China 57
China Institute in America 43
Chinese Immigration Act of 1924 21
Chinese Information Service 43
Chow, S.K. 43
Cicognani, A.G., Cardinal 43
Citadel 43, 57
Civilian Advisory Panel on Military Manpower Procurement 43
Clark, J.J. 43
Clark, Joan M. 43
Clark, Mark W. 22, 24, 26, 34, 43
Clarke, Brien 22
Clay, Lucius D. 17, 26, 34, 43, 57
Clayton, William L. 26
Clemens, Cyril 43
Cleveland, Harlan 43
Clifford, Clark 43
Cline, Ray S. 43
Clock, Philip 43
Close, Mrs. Edward B. 43
Coblentz, Gaston 16
Coburn, John B. 43
Coffey, Mathew B. 43

Colby, William E.	43
Cole, Felix	22, 24
Columbia Broadcasting System	43
Columbia University	43
Commission on the Organization of the Government for the Conduct of Foreign Policy	56
Connally, John B.	43
Cooke, Terence Cardinal	43
Cooper, John Sherman	43
Cootes, Merritt N.	43
Corcoran, Thomas G.	43
Cordier, Andrew W.	43
Corning Glass Works	43
Corrigan, Robert F.	34, 43
Cors, Allan	43
Cort, Stewart S.	43
Coster, Donald Q.	43
Council of Foreign Ministers	29
Council of the Americas	43
Council on Foreign Relations	43, 57
Cowen, Myron	34
Craigie, Robert A.P.	43
Cramer, Benjamin	34
Cramer, Robert	43
Crane, Katherine	16
Cronan, Richard J.	26, 34
Cronk, Edwin M.	43
Cross, Cecil M.P.	43
Crowe, Philip	34
Crowley, Leo	22
Csapski, Americ	43
Csonka, Emil	43
Culbert, Frederick P.	22, 26
Culbertson, Paul	22
Culbertson, William	34
Cummings, Nathan	34, 43
Czapski, Emeric	34
D'Esterno, Mira	34
Dainelli, Luca	43
Dakar	21, 24
Dana, William H.	43
Darlan, Admiral Jean	23
Darlan, Alain	34
Darlan-Boisson-Eisenhower Agreement, December 7, 1942	23
Darlan-Clark Agreement, November 22, 1942	23
Davies, A. Hudson	43
Davies, John Paton	17, 34
Davies, Joseph	26
Davies, Rodger P.	44
Davis, Monnett B.	22
Davis, Nathaniel	44

Davis, Norman ...22
Davis, Russell H., Jr. ...44
Davis, Thomas J., III ...44
Dawson, William ...22, 44
Deak, Francis ...34
Dean, Arthur ...44
DeButts, John D. ...44
DeCastro, Ralph ...34
Declaration of Atlantic Unity ...44
DeCourcy, William C. ...26
Dedijer, S. ...44
DeFreitas, Dick ...44
Dellisante, Philip ...44
DeLorenzo, Anthony ...44
Dennison, Charles S. ...44
Deutch, Michael J. ...44
Deverall, Richard ...34
Dewey, Thomas ...44
Dickey, Charles D. ...44
Diebold, John ...44
Dillon, Douglas ...44
Diplomatic and Consular Officers, Ret. (DACOR) ...43
Dobyns, Thomas G. ...34
Dombroski, Theresa ...44
Dominican Republic ...57
Donaldson, John W. ...44
Donhauser, Robert ...44
Donovan, William J. ...22, 26, 34
Doolittle, J.H. ...34
Dooman, Eugene ...35
Dorange, General ...44
Dorn, Frank ...35
Dorschner, John ...44
Doubleday Corporation ...44
Douglas, Lewis W. ...26, 35, 44
Douglas, William O. ...35
Douro, Richard ...44
Doyle, Albert M. ...35
Draper, W.H., Jr. ...26
Draper, William ...35
Dressendorfer, John H. ...44
Drummond, Roscoe ...16
Drumright, Everett ...35
Ducas, John J. ...44
Dulles, Allen ...26, 35
Dulles, Eleanor Lansing ...44
Dulles, John Foster ...10, 18, 26, 35
Dulles, Mrs. John Foster ...44
Dunn, James C. ...22, 26, 35, 44
Duranton, Roger ...35, 44
Durbrow, Elbridge ...26, 35, 44
Durkee, William P. ...44

Eagleburger, Lawrence S.	44
Eban, Abba	44
Economic cooperation - U.S. and Germany	32
Eisenhower, David	44
Eisenhower, Dwight D.	22, 26, 35, 38, 44, 57
Eisenhower, John	44
Eisenhower, Milton	35, 44
Elbrick, C. Burke	35, 44
Emmerich, Franz	44
Emmerson, John K.	35
Emmet, Christopher	44
Engelhard, Jane	44
Erhardt, John G.	22
Estes, Thomas S.	35, 44
Esteva, Georges	26
Europe	25
European Advisory Commission	32
Europeans in North Africa	23
Fahey, Daniel	35
Fair Campaign Practices Committee	44
Fairbanks, Douglas	35
Fairbanks, Douglas, Jr.	44
Fales, Rose H.	44
Far East-America Council	45, 57
Farish, Paul	22
Farland, Joseph S.	45
Farley, James A.	26, 35, 45
Fashek, Norman L.	45
Ferrari, Frank	45
Field, Noel	32
Figueroa, Sergio	45
Finch, Robert	45
Finn, Richard B.	45
Flandin, Pierre	32
Flanigan, Peter M.	45
Folger, John Clifford	45
Forbes, Malcolm S.	45
Ford, Gerald	45
Ford, Henry, II	45
Ford, Thomas	45
Foreign Intelligence Advisory Board	58
Foreign Policy Association	45
Foreign Reports	45
Foreign service	21
Foreign Service Journal	45
Forlani, Arnaldo	45
Former Members of Congress	45
Forrestal, James V.	22, 27
Fortas, Abe	45
Fowler, Henry H.	45
France	25, 32
France-America Society	57

```
Franco-Italian Accords ................................................25
Frankel, Max .........................................................45
Franklin, William M. .................................................45
Fredericks, J. Wayne .................................................45
Freedom House ........................................................45
Freeman, Orville L. ..................................................45
French National Committee (Free French) ..............................25
French officials in North Africa .....................................23
French propaganda ....................................................25
French-German Armistice ..............................................25
Friedrich, Harald ....................................................45
Friends of Free China ................................................45
Fukuda, Takeo ........................................................45
Fulbright, J. William ................................................45
Fullerton, Hugh .....................................................22, 27, 35, 45
Fund for Peace .......................................................57
Funk, Arthur L. ..................................................35, 45
Galbo, Vincent J. ....................................................45
Galbraith, John K. ...................................................27
Gallagher, Wes .......................................................45
Gallman, W.J. ........................................................45
Gandilhon, J. ........................................................45
Gardner, John ........................................................45
Gardner, Richard .....................................................45
Garin, Vasco Vieira ..................................................45
Garner, Robert L. ....................................................45
Garrett, Richard .....................................................45
Gates, Jack ..........................................................45
Gates, Thomas S. .....................................................45
Gaulle, Charles de ...................................................25
Gavin, James .........................................................45
Geliot, Christian ....................................................45
Gellhorn, Martha .....................................................27
Geopolitics ..........................................................57
George C. Marshall Research Foundation ...........................45, 57
George Washington University .........................................45
Gerhardt, H.A. .......................................................46
German American Chamber of Commerce ..................................46
German-French Armistice Agreement, June 22, 1940 .....................21
Germany ..................................................25, 30-32, 38
Gerten, Nicholas .....................................................27
Gibson, Hugh .....................................................27, 35
Gilbert, Carl J. .....................................................46
Gilchrist, Andrew and Ella ...........................................46
Gillan, T.M. .........................................................46
Giraud, Henri ................................................22, 25, 27
Glover, Cato .........................................................35
Godley, G. McMurtrie .................................................46
Goethals, Georges ....................................................27
Goldberg, Arthur J. ..................................................46
Goldman, Guido .......................................................46
```

Goldstern, Norbert .46
Goldwater, Barry .57
Goodpaster, A.J. .46
Gossett, Elizabeth .46
Goulli, Slaheddine el .46
Gowen, Franklin C. .46
Grace, J. Peter .46
Graham, Robert A. .46
Gray, Cecil .27
Great Britain .25
Greece .57
Green, Marshall .46
Greenwood, E.M. .35, 46
Grew, Joseph C. .27, 35
Gribanov .27
Griffin, Merv .18
Gromand, Roger .46
Gross, Ernest A. .27, 35
Gruber, Karl .57
Gruenther, Alfred M. .22, 27, 35
Gruson, Sydney .46
Guichard, Louis .22
Guiringaud, L. de .46
Gutheil, Helmut .46
Habib, Philip C. .46
Hagedorn, George C. .46
Hahn, H.P. .46
Haider, Michael .46
Haig, Alexander .46
Haight, G.W. .46
Halaby, Najeeb E. .46
Hall, William O. .46
Halsey, James H. .46
Hamilton, Maxwell .22
Hammarskjold, Dag .35
Handley, William J. .46
Handy, Thomas .35
Hanfstaengl, Egon .46
Hanser, Richard .20, 46
Harder, Howard .46
Hardy, Simone .27
Harley, F.L. .27
Harlow, Bryce .46
Harman, Phillip .46
Harnischfeger, Walter .27
Harriman, W. Averell .27, 46
Harrington, Julian .35
Harris, David .27
Harrop, William C. .46
Hartley, Livingston .46
Hartwell, Samuel A. .46
Harvey, Mose L. .18

Hauge, Gabriel	46
Hayes, Carlton J.H.	22
Hays, Brooks	46
Heath, Donald R.	46
Heberle, Jean-Claude	46
Heinz, Henry II	46
Heiskell, Andrew	46
Helms, Richard	46
Henderson, Loy	35
Henrikson, Alan K.	47
Henry-Haye, G.	27, 47
Henry-Haye, Pierre	22
Herbert, Roscoe	22
Herter, Christian A.	35, 47
Herzog, Mrs. Yaacov	47
Hesburgh, Theodore M.	47
Hibbard, Frederick	22
Hickerson, John	27, 35
Hicks, John F.G.	47
Higgins, Frank	35
Higgins, Marguerite	35
Hight, John W.	47
Hill, Robert C.	47
Hillenbrand, Martin J.	47
Hillenkoetter, R.H.	35
Hinds, A. Boyd	47
Hinton, Longstreet	47
Hirsch, Henri L.	25
Hitler, Adolf	31-32
Hobby, Oveta Culp	35
Hoffman, Paul G.	35, 47
Hoisington, William A., Jr.	47
Holmes, Julius C.	22, 27
Hoopes, Townsend	47
Hoover, Herbert C.	22, 27, 35
Hoover, Herbert, Jr.	35, 47
Hoover, J. Edgar	35
Hopkins, Harry	27
Hopper, Bruce C.	47
Horkan, George A.	47
Hottelet, Richard	47
Hotung, Eric	47
Houghton, Amory	18, 35, 47, 57
Houghton, Amory, Jr.	35
Houghton, Arthur A., Jr.	47
Housman, Richard Jay	47
Howe, George	35
Howley, Frank L.	47
Hoxie, R. Gordon	47
Hoxter, Curtis J.	47
Hrones, John G.	22, 27, 47

Hsiung, James C.	47
Hughes, Charles E.	21
Hughes, Thomas L.	47
Hulick, Charles	27
Hull, Cordell	22, 25, 27, 35
Humes, John P.	47
Humphrey, Hubert	47
Hungary	25
Hunter, Edward	47
Hurley, Patrick	25
Huston, Cloyce	22
Ignatieff, Alex	47
Independent League for European Cooperation	33
Indochina	25
Ingersoll, Robert S.	47
Institute of International Education	47
Intelligence service	58
Inter-Allied relations	23
Inter-Allied Reparations Agency	29
International economic relations	58
International Executive Service Corps	47, 58
International Management and Development Institute	47
International relations	38
International Rescue Committee	47
International Telephone and Telegraph Company	47
Irvine, Reed J.	47
Irwin, John	47
Israeli-Arab settlement	38
Italian armistice	59
Italy	58
Italy - Allied Advisory Council	25
Jackson, Henry M.	47
Jacobs, Joseph	27
Janeway, Eliot	47
Japan	58
Japan America Institute	47
Japan American Cultural Society	47
Japan Fund	48, 58
Japan International Christian University Foundation	48
Japan National Student Association	48
Japan Society	48, 58
Jessup, Philip	27
Jews - Repatriation	25
Johari, Gyan	48
Johnson, Lyndon B.	48, 58
Johnson, Mrs. Lyndon B.	48
Johnson, U. Alexis	36, 48
Johnston, Eric	36
Jolly, Edwin J.	58
Jones, Harry W.	48
Jones, Howard P.	36
Jones, J. Wesley	27
Jones, James	48

Jones, Roger W. 48
Jousse, General 48
Judd, Walter H. 48
Kalicki, J.H. 20
Kaspi, Andre 48
Kearns, Henry 48
Keating, Kenneth 48
Keeley, James H. 36
Kelly, John E. 48
Kelsey, John W., Jr. 48
Kennan, George F. 27, 36, 48
Kennedy, Edward M. 48
Kennedy, John and Jacqueline 36, 48
Kennedy, Joseph P. 36
Kennedy, Mrs. Joseph 48
Kennedy, Robert F. 48
Kern, Harry F. 48
Kerr, Walter 48
Kessler, Frank 48
Keyes, Geoffrey 27
Khan, Najmul Saqib 48
Kim, Young Sun 48
King, David 27
King, Wunsz 36
Kirk, Alexander 22, 25, 36
Kissinger, Henry 21, 48
Klein, Julius 48
Kline, Hugh 48
Knapp, J. Burke 27, 48
Knight, Ridgway B. 48
Knoppers, Antonie T. 48
Knowlton, William A. 48
Knox, John 48
Knox, William 48
Kocher, Eric 36
Koehler, John O. 48
Kohlberg, Alfred 36
Kohler, Foy D. 48
Kolko, Gabriel 48
Korry, Edward M. 48
Koubbi, Albert el 48
Krantz, Frederick 27
Krantz, Marian 27
Kraus, Maria 48
Krock, Arthur 48
Kuhn, Irene Corbally 48
Kupferman, Theodore 48
LaFollette, Charles D. 27, 49
Laird, Melvin R. 49
Lamont, Thomas S. 49, 58
Land, Edwin H. 49
Lane, Arthur Bliss 22

```
Langer, William .............................................................27, 49
Lapeyre, Andre ..................................................................25
Lasky, Melvin J. ................................................................49
Latimer, Thomas K. ..............................................................49
Laukhuff, Perry .............................................................27, 36
Launay, J.F. de .................................................................49
Lazrus, Oscar M. ................................................................49
League of Americans Residing Abroad .............................................49
Leahy, William D. .......................................................22, 27, 36
Lebanon .........................................................................38
Lehaney, Francis ................................................................49
Lehmann, Manfred R. .............................................................49
Lemaigre-Dubreuil, Jacques ..............................................22, 25, 27
Lemaigre-Dubreuil, Jean-Pierre ..................................................49
LeMay, Curtis ...................................................................27
Lemnitzer, L.L. .................................................................49
Leonard, Richard G. .............................................................49
Leonhart, William ...............................................................49
Levy-Despas, Andre ..............................................................49
Lewis, Joseph ...................................................................49
Li, K.T. ........................................................................49
Li, Mo ..........................................................................49
Library of Presidential Papers ..................................................49
Lichtenstein, Walter ............................................................36
Likeman, J.L. ...................................................................27
Lilienthal, David E. ............................................................49
Lindsay, Franklin A. ............................................................49
Lindsay, John V. ................................................................49
Lloyd, Alan .....................................................................19
Lodge, Henry Cabot ..........................................................36, 49
Lodge, John Davis ...........................................................36, 49
Lodigensky, A.A. ................................................................49
Loeb, John L. ...................................................................49
Loh, I-Cheng ....................................................................49
Long, Breckinridge ..............................................................27
Longworth, Mrs. Nicholas ........................................................49
Loridan, Walter .................................................................49
Loughran, Jack ..................................................................49
Lovestone, Jay ..................................................................49
Lovett, Robert ..............................................................27, 49
Lowenthal, Abraham F. ...........................................................49
Lubbers, Arend P. ...............................................................49
Luce, Clare Boothe ..........................................................36, 49
Luce, Henry, III ................................................................49
Ludden, Raymond .................................................................49
Lynch, R.J. .....................................................................49
Lynch, Robert ...................................................................27
Lyon, Cecil B. ..............................................................36, 49
Lyon, Frederick B. ..............................................................27
MacArthur, Douglas, II ..........................................23, 27, 36, 49
MacAvoy, Thomas C. ..............................................................49
```

MacLeish, Archibald	27
Macmillan, Harold	23, 27, 36, 49
Macomber, William B., Jr.	49
MacVeagh, Lincoln	23
Magruder, Carter	27
Mahoney, James P.	49
Maillard, William S.	49
Mallory, L.D.	23
Manning, Bayliss	49
Mansfield, Mike	36, 50
Marcos, Imelda	50
Marie Salvatora, Sister	50
Marquette University	50
Marshall Plan	58
Marshall, George	23, 28, 36
Martin, Graham A.	50
Martin, William McC., Jr.	50
Marwell, David G.	50
Massigli, Rene	23
Mast, Charles	23, 50
Mast, L.	28
Mathias, Charles Mc., Jr.	50
Matthews, H. Freeman	23, 28, 36
May, Dick	50
Mayer, Charles T.	50
Mayer, Ernest de W.	23
McBride, Robert	50
McCarthy, Frank	28, 50
McChrystal, Arthur J.	50
McClelland, Roswell	36
McClintock, Robert	21, 36, 50
McCloy, John J.	28, 36
McCloy, John J., II	50
McClure, Robert	23
McCone, John A.	50
McCormick, Ken	36, 50
McDowell, Robert H.	50
McFall, Jack K.	50
McFarland, Joseph B.	50
McGhee, George C.	50
McGraw, James	28
McGregor, Robert G.	50
McGuire, Perkins	36
McIlvaine, Robinson	50
McIntyre, J.M.	50
McMahon, William	50
McNamara, Robert S.	50
Meany, George	50
Mefret, Noel	28, 50
Melandri, Pierre	50
Melbourne, Roy M.	50
Menjou, Adolphe	23

Menuhin, Moshe	50
Menuhin, Yehudi	36, 50
Menzies, Prime Minister	9
Menzies, Robert G.	50
Merchant, Livingston	50
Merigeault, Rene	28
Merrill, Eugene	36
Mesta, Perle	36, 58
Meyer, Armin	50
Meyer, Charles A.	50
Meyer, Frank	50
Meyer, John M., Jr.	50
Miao, P.C.	28
Michiko, Princess	16
Middendorf, J. William, II	50
Middle East	38
Middleton, George	36
Milburn, Bryan	50
Military Government Conference, August, 1945	33
Millard, Hugh	36
Miller, Gething C.	50
Millington-Drake, Eugen	50
Mineral industries	25
Miranda, Francisco de	25
Moellering, John H.	50
Molotov, V.M.	30
Mommsen, Ernst Wolf	50
Monnet, Jean	50
Montrichard, de	23
Moore, John D.J.	50
Moore, Walden	51
Moorer, Thomas H.	51
Morgan Guaranty Trust Company	16, 51, 58
Moro, Aldo	51
Morris, Brewster	36
Moscow Conference, October, 1943	24
Mountbatten, The Earl of	51
Moynihan, Daniel P.	51
Mulligan, Dennis J.	51
Mundt, Karl E.	51
Murphy, Charles J.V.	51
Murphy, Gavin	51
Murphy, Raymond	28
Murphy, Richard W.	51
Murphy, Robert D., Jr.	51
Murphy, Thomas A.	51
Murphy, Wallace	23
Nabokoff, Nicolas	28
Nagorski, Zygmunt	51
Nakashima, Nobuyuki	51
Nakasone, Yasuhiro	51
Nara, Yasuhiko	51
National Association of Manufacturers	51

National Conference of Christians and Jews 51, 58
National Export Expansion Council 58
National Foreign Trade Council 51
National Planning Association 51, 58
Neff, John C. 51
Nehru, B.K. 51
Nelson, Walter Henry 51
Newman, James 28
Newsom, David D. 51
Newton, Henry 51
Nitze, Paul H. 51
Nixon, Patricia 51
Nixon, Richard M. 19, 36, 51
Nizer, Louis 28
Norden, Carl 25, 51
Norris, Robert B. 51
Norstad, Lauris 36, 51
North Africa 24-25
North African and French West African Accords 24
North African Campaign 24
North African Economic Board 28, 36, 58
Norton, Edward J. 23
Nuveen, John 36
O'Brien, John A. 51
O'Brien, William G. 23, 28, 36, 51
O'Connor, Roderic 51
O'Donnell, E.J. 36
Oehlert, B.H., Jr. 51
Oestreicher, Sylvan 36, 51
Office of the Military Government of the United States (OMGUS) 30
Offie, Carmel 23, 28, 36, 51
Okazaki, Eimatsu 36
Okazaki, Katsuo 36
Onassis, Aristotle 51
Operation TORCH 24
Oppenheimer, Franz M. 51
Oppenheimer, Fritz 28, 36
Osborn, David 51
Overby, Andrew N. 51
Ovidio, Antonio d' 51
Pace, Frank, Jr. 36
Packard, David 51
Packer, Earl L. 51
Pakistan Cyclone Relief Fund 58
Paley, William S. 51
Palmer, Ely 37
Paris American Club 52
Parks, Robert B. 52
Parsons, Jeanne 52
Pasquet, Mme. Maurice 52
Pasquier, Pierre du 23, 28, 52
Pasquier, Verena du 52
Patton, George 28

Pauley, Edwin W.	28
Pauphilet, B.	52
Peale, Norman Vincent	52
Pearson, Lester	52
Pedersen, Richard F.	52
Pendar, Kenneth	28
Perkins, Richard	52
Peterfi, William O.	52
Petersen, Howard C.	52
Petree, Virginia H.	52
Petrov, Vladimir	18, 52
Peurifoy, John	28
Philpott, Robert J.	52
Phleger, Herman	52
Picot, Willy George	52
Pinay, Antoine	52
Pinkley, Virgil	28, 52
Pius XIII	16
Platzner, Wilfried	37
Plaza, Galo	52
Plimpton, Francis T.P.	52
Plitt, James R.	52
Pogue, Forrest	37
Polk, Mrs. Judd N.	52
Pollock, James	28
Poole, DeWitt	28
Pope, Maurice	28
Popper, David H.	52
Porter, Dwight J.	52
Porter, William J.	52
Potter, Gary	52
Presidential Transition Committee	39
Prochnow, Herbert V.	52
Prohibition	21
Project Hope	58
Protter, Benjamin	52
Prud'homme, Hector	28
Psychological warfare	25
Public Advisory Committee for Trade Negotiations	58
Rabb, Maxwell M.	52
Rabin, Yitzhak	52
Radford, Arthur W.	37, 52
Radio Free Europe	58
Radvanyi, Janos	52
Raghavan, Jai D.	52
Ramsbotham, Peter	52
Ramsey, James	52
Randshuysen, Gerard	23
Rankin, Karl	37
Raymond, Arthur J.	37
Read, Benjamin H.	52
Reber, Samuel	23, 28, 37
Rees, David	52

Reid, Ogden	37
Reid, W. Stafford	52
Reischauer, Edwin O. and Haru	52
Repin, Ilya	38
Republican National Committee	52
Reston, James	52
Reuter, Ernst	16
Rhee, Syngman	37
Rheinstrom, H.	37
Rhoade, Max	21
Ribbentrop, Joachim von	30
Ribicoff, Abraham	52
Rice, Louis J., Jr.	52
Richardson, Elliot L.	52
Riddleberger, James W.	28, 37, 52
Ridgway, Matthew B.	37, 52
Riess, Curt	53
Roach, Perry	53
Robertson, Walter	37
Roche, James M.	53
Rockefeller Public Service Awards	53
Rockefeller, David	53
Rockefeller, James S.	53
Rockefeller, John D., III	37, 53
Rockefeller, Mr. and Mrs. Nelson A.	53
Rockwell, Stuart W.	53
Rogers, William P.	53
Rolling Stone	53
Romney Associates	53
Romney, George	53
Romulo, Carlos	37, 53
Rooney, Catherine	53
Rooney, John J.	53
Roosevelt, Eleanor	28, 37
Roosevelt, Franklin D.	25, 28, 32
Rose, France de	37
Rosenberg, Elliot	53
Rositzke, Harry	53
Rostow, Eugene V.	53
Rostow, Walt W.	28, 53
Roudakoff, Paul	53
Rountree, William M.	53
Rowan, Leslie	53
Rowney, E.	53
Royall, Kenneth	28, 37
Rubloff, Arthur	53
Rubottom, R. Richard, Jr.	53
Rueff, Jacques	53
Rueger, William F.	53
Ruhr	32
Ruhr-Rhineland	29
Rumsfeld, Donald H.	53

Rush, Kenneth	53
Rusk, Dean	28, 37, 53
Russell, Donald	28
Russell, H. Earle	23
Russell, Mrs. Irving	53
Russell, Richard	23
Russia - History	38
Rutledge, Campbell, Jr.	53
Saar	29
Saccio, Leonard J.	53
Safire, William	53
Saint Hardouin, Jacques T. de	28
Saltonstall, Leverett	53
Saltzman, Charles E.	28, 53
Samuels, Nathaniel	53
Sandusky, Michael C.	53
Sarnoff, Robert W.	53
Sato, Eisaku	19, 53
Satterthwaite, Joseph C.	53
Sause, Mrs. Oliver	53
Scali, John A.	53
Schaefer, Steve	53
Scheuer, Sidney H.	53
Schlesinger, James R.	53
Schmidt, Helmut	53
Schneider, Douglas	28
Schott, William W.	23
Schulenberg, Friedrich von	30
Scott, Hugh	54
Scott, John	54
Scranton, William M.	54
Scribner, Fred C., Jr.	54
Seaborg, Glenn T.	54
Searle, William A.	54, 58
Sebald, William J.	37
Seeds, Robert	54
Seignious, George M., II	54
Senoussi, Badreddine	54
Sevareid, Eric	28
Shah, Konsin C.	54
Shaine, H.B.	54
Shaw, G. Howland	23, 28
Sheean, Mrs. Vincent	54
Sheean, Vincent	37
Sheehan, John E.	54
Shepley, James R.	54
Shirer, William	23
Shoji, Keijiro	54
Shriver, R. Sargent, Jr.	54
Shultz, George	54
Simon, Eugene	54
Simon, William E.	54

Simpson, Smith	19
Singer, Herbert	54
Sisco, Joseph J.	54
Skouras, Spyros	37
Smalley, Walter	54
Smith, Bernard	37
Smith, Carleton	54
Smith, Gerard C.	54
Smith, James S.	54
Smith, Richard J.	54
Smith, Richard W.	54
Smith, W. Bedell	23, 28, 37
Sneider, Richard L.	54
Societe Anonyme Belge D'Exploitation de la Navigation Aerienne (SABENA)	54
Soffer, Elie	54
Solborg, Robert	23
Soong Mei-ling	43
Soustelle, Jacques	54
Spain	25
Spellman, Francis Cardinal	28, 37, 54
Spivak, Lawrence	54
Spofford, Charles	28
Springer, Axel	54
Stabler, Wells	54
Staercke, Andre de	54
Standish, Myles	54
Stans, Maurice	54
Stanton, Frank	54
Stassen, Harold	37
Steedman, Alec	37, 54
Steelman, John	28
Steeves, John M.	37, 54
Stegmaier, John L.	54
Steingut, Leo	28
Stephens, Dorsey	23
Stephens, John W.	54
Stettinius, Edward	23, 25
Stettinius, Edward, Jr.	28
Stevens, Robert	37, 54
Stevenson, Adlai	37
Stimson, Henry	28
Stoessel, Walter	54
Stone, Donald	28
Stone, Galen L.	54
Stone, William E.	28
Strang, William	29
Straus, Jesse	32
Straus, Oscar S., II	54
Straus, Ralph I.	55
Strauss, Lewis L.	55
Strausz-Hupe, Robert	55
Struelens, Michel	55

Sugahara, K.	55
Sullivan, Joseph T.P.	55
Sulzberger, Arthur H.	37
Sulzberger, Arthur Ochs	55
Sumner, Edward	29
Sun Yun-suan	55
Surrey Probation Area	55
Swope, Herbert Bayard	29
Symington, W. Stuart	29, 55
Szymczak, M.S.	29
Taft, Orray, Jr.	37
Taft, Philip	20, 55
Tait, George	23
Tanaka, Mitsuo	37
Tanguy, Charles R.	55
Tasca, Henry	55
Taylor, Maxwell	29, 37
Teissier, Jacques	55
Tello, Manuel	55
Thai, Nguyen	55
Thayer, Sylvanus	20
Thompson, Mr. and Mrs. Llewellyn	55
Thompson, Tyler	37
Tittmann, Harold H.	37
Togo, Fumihiko	55
Tomabechi, T.	55
Tong, Hollington	37
Tordella, Dr.	58
Torrente, Henry de	37
Torres, Baron de las	55
Tournaire, J.A.	55
Trebesch, Herbert	55
Tresize, Philip	55
Trieste	30
Trilateral Commission	55
Tripartite Talks, London	32
Trizonia	32
Trowbridge, A.B.	55
Truitt, Max	37
Truman, Harry	29, 37
Tuck, S. Pinkney	23, 29
Tully, Grace	29
Turner, Stansfield	55
Turner, William C.	55
Tute, Warren	55
Tuthill, John W.	29, 55
Twining, Nathan	55
Twitchell, Kenaston	55
U.S. - Economic relations - Germany	21
U.S. Department of State	29
U.S.-French negotiations	24
U.S.S.R.	25
Ungerer, Werner	55

Union of Soviet Socialist Republics	33
United Nations	30, 38
United Nations Association of the United States of America	55, 58
United States	25, 33, 38, 58
United States Committee for Refugees	58
United States Council	55
United States Council of the International Chamber of Commerce	55, 58
United States Korea Economic Council	55
United States Mission to the United Nations	55
United States Office of Srategic Services	24
United States Overseas Information and Cultural Program	58
University Club	55
Upston, John E.	55
Ushiba, Nobuhiko	55
Vailati, Vanna	55
Van Heck, Paul	23
Vance, Cyrus	55
Vandenberg, Arthur H.	29
Vaughn, Harry	29
Vernon, Raymond	55
Veterans of Foreign Wars	55
Viorst, Milton	18
Voice of America	33
Volcker, Paul A.	55
Voorhees, Tracy	37
Vuillien, Charles	29
Vyshinsky, Andrei	23, 29
Wailes, Edward	20, 37
Wallin, Paul J.	56
Wallner, Woodruff	29
Walmsley, Walter N.	56
Wang Li-yen	58
War correspondents	25
Wasson, Thomas	23
Watson, H.	23
Watson, Thomas J., Jr.	56
Watts, W. Walter	56
Watts, William	56
Waugh, Samuel C.	56
Webb, James E.	29, 37, 56
Wedemeyer, Albert C.	37, 56
Weinstein, Martin E.	56
Weisbrod, Ray	56
Wells, Gladys	37
Weygand, Jacques	29
Weygand, Maxime	23-24, 37
Weyl, Nathaniel	56
Whitcomb, Philip W.	56
White, Thomas	38
Whitehouse, Charles S.	56
Whitman, Ann C.	56
Wickersham, Neil	29

Wiley, Alexander 56
Wiley, John C. 38
Wilkinson, Burke 17
Williams, Jack S. 38
Williams, Margaret 38
Williams, Walter 38
Willis, Frances 38
Winant, John 23
Withers, William 18
Woll, Matthew 9
Wood, John 38
Woods, Rose Mary 56
Woodward, Robert 38
Woodyear, William 38
World Rehabilitation Fund 58
World Trade Fair, Yugoslavia 58
World War I 25
World War II 25
Wright, Jerauld 38, 56
Wriston, Henry 56
Wyden, Peter H. 56
Wyman, Thomas H. 56
Yamazaki, Toshio 56
Yasukawa, Takeshi 56
Yeh, George 56
Yen, C.K. 56
Yokoyama, Soichi 20
Yosano, Shigeru 38
Yoshida, Shigeru 38
Yost, Charles W. 56
Young, Kenneth 38
Young, R.A. 56
Zablocki, Clement J. 56
Zahedi, Ardeshir 56
Zahn, Joachim 56
Zakaria, H.M.A. 56
Zanuck, Darryl F. 56
Zayas, Alfred M. de 56
Zorlu, Fatin Rusto 56
Zurhellen, J. Owen, Jr. 56